CiRCUiTRY

The complete guide to Circuits,
Channels and Gates

by Richard Rudd
with contributions from Judy Dendy

GENE KEYS

This edition published in Great Britain and USA 2021
by Gene Keys Publishing Ltd
Lytchett House, 13 Freeland Park
Wareham Road, Lytchett Matravers, Poole BH16 6FA

Richard Rudd

CIRCUITRY
The complete guide to Circuits, Channels and Gates

Hardback Edition ISBN: 978-1-9996710-5-1
Kindle ISBN: 978-1-8380487-9-2

genekeys.com

THE COMPLETE GUIDE TO CIRCUITS, CHANNELS AND GATES

PREFACE

It has been the task for many years to bring ease and succinctness to the understanding and practice of Human Design. Despite its depth and complexity, Design is logical. Its very logic holds the key to grasping and applying the knowledge's beauty and functionality. In training teachers of Rave Cartography, I have emphasised the basic A B C's – the foundation concepts that ensure a true grasp of one's Human Design.

A is for Personality and Design, B is for Hexagram Line structure and C is for Circuits and Channels. A brings understanding to the inner human dynamic between the accessible personality and the surprising unconscious. B lays the foundation for Line and Profile analysis. It is C alone which deals with the actual structure and dynamics of the Bodygraph itself. It is the matrix upon which the differentiated self is revealed.

Richard Rudd has a great gift of distilling complex material into readable and insightful prose. This work on Channels and Circuits is an important contribution in better understanding the Human Design System.

Ra Uru Hu
Ibiza, Spain
11 June 2003

AUTHOR'S NOTE

Anyone who knows the Human Design System also knows that it is a veritable minefield for the newcomer. Added to this, the system is still new enough to be under constant research and scrutiny by so many of the students who have become involved in it. Like the human beings it describes, Human Design is a mutative knowledge – constantly changing, developing and adapting as it meets all kinds of new minds who test it and shape it to meet the growing needs of the world.

Human Design has begun its life as a fringe science, whether those involved in it like it or not. Its unusual origins and the esoteric nature of its subject material have placed it in a category where it truly does not belong. That is to say, Human Design is not only for the esoteric, but contains simple truths that can be so helpful to so many human beings in the world at large. But if the world at large is to hear about Human Design, one of the first things that must happen is that the language in which it is transmitted should be clear and simple.

This book intends to present some of the concepts of Human Design in a simple and practical way. It has come about as a response to the needs of both students and laypeople who take an interest in the system. I hope it will help and inspire people to understand both themselves and those around them in the world.

Richard Rudd

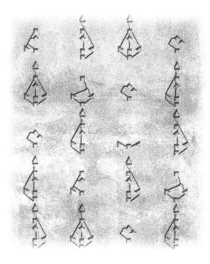

TABLE OF CONTENTS

PART 1

PART 2

PART 1

THE CIRCUITS

Beneath the Human Design Bodygraph lies a labyrinth of detail and symmetry. It is actually possible to look into a single gate and derive a basic 56,160 possible permutations within the way in which it operates. But as with Theseus' mythic journey, there is a golden thread that can lead us through the labyrinth and bring us out on the other side without becoming lost.

This thread in Human Design is known as Circuitry. There are a total of six separate basic circuits within the bodygraph plus the four channels known as the Integration channels. Even though there are other specialised circuits hiding within the bodygraph (such as the two mystical circuits – the microcosmic circuit (four channels) and the macrocosmic circuit (WA) (six channels)), the six basic circuits underpin the entire operation of a human being. They describe the deepest genetic processes that drive our species, and as such they allow us to view each other as different parts of a totality in a wholly impersonal way.

If one were to know only the circuits in Human Design without knowing anything at all about the channels and gates, one could do a profound and penetrating analysis of any Human Design chart. If the bodygraph were a building, the circuits would be the architect's blueprints. When you discover which circuit or circuits dominate in your design, it clearly shows not only your genetic wiring and predispositions in life, but also what and whom it is you are seeking outside yourself to bring a sense of fulfilment. It is very rare that an individual completes an entire circuit (with the exception of the 2 minor circuits), which illustrates well how conditioned we are to seek out the correct allies in life.

Below are the main keynotes of Human Design circuitry. It is well to bear in mind that most human beings have a mixture of circuitry defined in their design, and thus the keynotes and concepts given need to be seen in the context of the whole of one's design. Synthesising all this information requires skill, training and above all time.

Those who are interested in learning how to use this information at a professional level are invited to contact your national Human Design organisation and ask for details of the many training programmes that are available.

INDEX OF CHANNELS, GATES AND THEIR KEYNOTES

Below is a complete index of the master keynotes for every channel and gate in the Human Design bodygraph. The name of each channel and gate is written in black and in the case of the gates, these are drawn from the original headings from the traditional I Ching. The keynotes of each channel and gate can also be seen below each heading, highlighted in blue. In advanced Human Design analysis, these keynotes can be strung together to create themes and stories that reflect the behavioural patterns in our lives.

Taking the simplest example of the *1st gate*, you can see the name of this gate is *The Creative*, and you could say that someone with this whole channel *(1 - 8)* in their design – the channel of **Inspiration** – is designed to be *a creative role model* who is here to make their *contribution* through *self expression*.

Gate & Keynote		Harmonic Gate & Keynote		Channel & Keynote	
1	The Creative Self expression	8	Holding Together Contribution	1 - 8	Inspiration A design of a creative role model
2	The Receptive The Direction of the Self	14	Possession in Great Measure Power Skills	2 - 14	The Beat A design of being keeper of the keys
3	Difficulty at the Beginning Ordering	60	Limitation Acceptance	3 - 60	Mutation A design of energy which fluctuates and initiates, pulse
4	Youthful Folly Formulisation	63	After Completion Doubt	63 - 4	Logic A design of mental ease mixed with doubt
5	Waiting Fixed Rhythms	15	Modesty Extremes	5 - 15	Rhythm A design of being in the flow
6	Conflict Friction	59	Dispersion Sexuality	59 - 6	Mating A design focused on reproduction
7	The Army The Role of the Self	31	Influence Leading	7 - 31	The Alpha A design of leadership for "good" or "bad"
8	Holding Together Contributions	1	The Creative Self Expression	1 - 8	Inspiration A design of a creative role model
9	The Taming Power of the Small Focus	52	Keeping Still Inaction	9 - 52	Concentration A design of determination, focused
10	Treading The behaviour of the self	20	Contemplation The Now	10 - 20	Awakening A design of commitment to higher principles
10	Treading The behaviour of the self	34	The Power of the Great Might	34 - 10	Exploration A design of following one's convictions
10	Treading The behaviour of the self	57	The Gentle Intuition	57 - 10	Perfected Form A design for survival

Gate & Keynote		Harmonic Gate & Keynote		Channel & Keynote	
11	Peace Ideas	56	The Wanderer Stimulation	11 - 56	Curiosity A design of a searcher
12	Standstill Caution	22	Grace Openness	22 - 12	Openness A design of a social being
13	The Fellowship of Man The Listener	33	Retreat Privacy	13 - 33	The Prodigal A design of a witness
14	Possession in Great Measure Power Skills	2	The Receptive The Direction of the Self	2 - 14	Beat A design of being keeper of the keys
15	Modesty Extremes	5	Waiting Fixed Rhythms	5 - 15	Rhythm A design of being in the flow
16	Enthusiasm Skills	48	The Well Depth	48 - 16	The Wavelength A design of talent
17	Following Opinions	62	Preponderance of the Small Detail	17 - 62	Acceptance A design of an organisational being
18	Work on what has been Spoilt Correction	58	The Joyous Aliveness	18 - 58	Judgement A design of insatiability
19	Approach Wanting	49	Revolution Rejection	19 - 49	Synthesis A design of sensitivity
20	Contemplation The Now	10	Treading The Behaviour of the Self	10 - 20	Awakening A design of commitment to higher principles
20	Contemplation The Now	34	The Power of the Great Might	34 - 20	Charisma A design where thoughts must become deeds
20	Contemplation The Now	57	The Gentle Intuition	57 - 20	The Brain Wave A design of penetrating awareness
21	Biting Through The Hunter, Huntress	45	Gathering Together The Gatherer	21 - 45	Money A design of a materialist
22	Grace Openness	12	Standstill Caution	22 - 12	Openness A design of a social being
23	Splitting Apart Assimilation	43	Breakthrough Insight	43 - 23	Structuring A design of individuality
24	Returning Rationalising	61	Inner Truth Mystery	61 - 24	Awareness A design of a thinker
25	Innocence The Spirit of the Self	51	The Arousing Shock	25 - 51	Initiation A design of needing to be first
26	The Taming Power of the Great The Egoist	44	Coming to Meet Alertness	44 - 26	Surrender A design of a transmitter
27	Nourishment Caring	50	The Cauldron Values	27 - 50	Preservation A design of custodianship
28	Preponderance of the Great The Game Player	38	Opposition The Fighter	38 - 28	Struggle A design of stubbornness

Gate & Keynote	Harmonic Gate & Keynote	Channel & Keynote
29 The Abysmal — Saying Yes	46 Pushing Upward — Determination	29 - 46 Discovery — A design of succeeding where others fail
30 Clinging Fire — Feelings	41 Decrease — Contraction	41 - 30 Recognition — A design of focused energy
31 Influence — Leading	7 The Army — The Role of the Self	7 - 31 The Alpha — A design of leadership for "good" or "bad"
32 Duration — Continuity	54 The Marrying Maiden — Ambition	54 - 32 Transformation — A design of being driven
33 Retreat — Privacy	13 The Fellowship of Man — The Listener	13 - 33 The Prodigal — A design of a witness
34 The Power of the Great — Might	10 Treading — The Behaviour of the Self	34 - 10 Exploration — A design of following one's convictions
34 The Power of the Great — Might	20 Contemplation — The Now	34 - 20 Charisma — A design where thoughts must become deeds
34 The Power of the Great — Might	57 The Gentle — Intuition	57 - 34 Power — A design of an archetype
35 Progress — Change	36 The Darkening of the Light — Crisis	35 - 36 Transitoriness — A design of being a Jack of all Trades
36 The Darkening of the Light — Crisis	35 Progress — Change	35 - 36 Transitoriness — A design of being a Jack of all Trades
37 The Family — Friendship	40 Deliverance — Aloneness	37 - 40 Community — A design of being a part seeking a whole
38 Opposition — The Fighter	28 Preponderance of the Great — The Game Player	38 - 28 Struggle — A design of stubbornness
39 Obstruction — The Provocateur	55 Abundance — Spirit	39 - 55 Emoting — A design of moodiness
40 Deliverance — Aloneness	37 The Family — Friendship	37 - 40 Community — A design of being a part seeking a whole
41 Decrease — Contraction	30 Clinging Fire — Feelings	41 - 30 Recognition — A design of focused energy
42 Increase — Growth	53 Development — Beginnings	53 - 42 Maturation — A design of balanced development, cyclic
43 Breakthrough — Insight	23 Splitting Apart — Assimilation	43 - 23 Structuring — A design of individuality
44 Coming to Meet — Alertness	26 The Taming Power of the Great — The Egoist	44 - 26 Surrender — A design of a transmitter
45 Gathering Together — The Gatherer	21 Biting Through — The Hunter, Huntress	21 - 45 Money — A design of a materialist
46 Pushing Upward — Determination	29 The Abysmal — Saying Yes	29 - 46 Discovery — A design of succeeding where others fail

Gate & Keynote		Harmonic Gate & Keynote		Channel & Keynote	
47	Oppression Realising	64	Before Completion Confusion	64 - 47	Abstraction A design of mental activity and clarity
48	The Well Depth	16	Enthusiasm Skills	48 - 16	The Wavelength A design of talent
49	Revolution Rejection	19	Approach Wanting	19 - 49	Synthesis A design of sensitivity
50	The Cauldron Values	27	Nourishment Caring	27 - 50	Preservation A design of custodianship
51	The Arousing Shock	25	Innocence The Spirit of the Self	25 - 51	Initiation A design of needing to be first
52	Keeping Still Inaction	9	The Taming Power of the Small Focus	9 - 52	Concentration A design of determination, focused
53	Development Beginnings	42	Increase Growth	53 - 42	Maturation A design of balanced development, cyclic
54	The Marrying Maiden Ambition	32	Duration Continuity	54 - 32	Transformation A design of being driven
55	Abundance Spirit	39	Obstruction The Provocateur	39 - 55	Emoting A design of moodiness
56	The Wanderer Stimulation	11	Peace Ideas	11 - 56	Curiosity A design of a searcher
57	The Gentle Intuition	10	Treading The behaviour of the self	57 - 10	Perfected Form A design for survival
57	The Gentle Intuition	20	Contemplation The Now	57 - 20	The Brain Wave A design of penetrating awareness
57	The Gentle Intuition	34	The Power of the Great Might	57 - 34	Power A design of an archetype
58	The Joyous Aliveness	18	Work on what has been Spoilt Correction	18 - 58	Judgement A design of insatiability
59	Dispersion Sexuality	6	Conflict Friction	59 - 6	Mating A design focused on reproduction
60	Limitation Acceptance	3	Difficulty at the Beginning Ordering	3 - 60	Mutation A design of energy which fluctuates and initiates, pulse
61	Inner Truth Mystery	24	Returning Rationalising	61 - 24	Awareness A design of a thinker
62	Preponderance of the Small Detail	17	Following Opinions	17 - 62	Acceptance A design of an organisational being
63	After Completion Doubt	4	Youthful Folly Formulisation	63 - 4	Logic A design of mental ease mixed with doubt
64	Before Completion Confusion	47	Oppression Realising	64 - 47	Abstraction A design of mental activity and clarity

THE THREE CIRCUIT GROUPS

The six circuits (excluding the Integration Channels) make up three circuit groups – *the Individual Circuit group*, *the Collective Circuit group* and *the Tribal Circuit group* – each of which has two circuits and a master keynote:

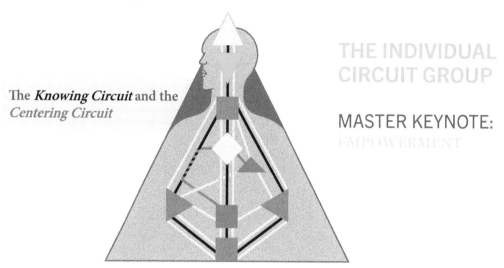

THE INDIVIDUAL
CIRCUIT GROUP

MASTER KEYNOTE:
EMPOWERMENT

The *Knowing Circuit* and the
Centering Circuit

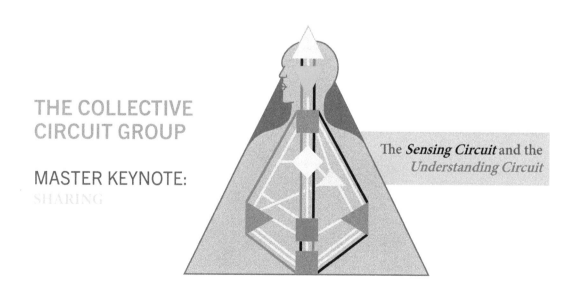

THE COLLECTIVE
CIRCUIT GROUP

MASTER KEYNOTE:
SHARING

The *Sensing Circuit* and the
Understanding Circuit

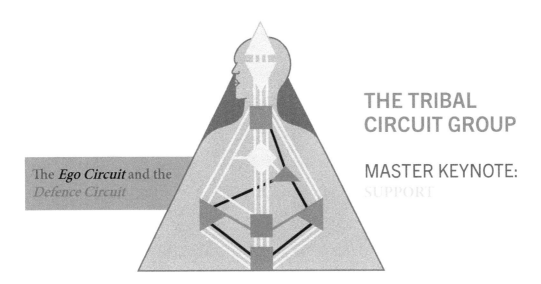

**THE TRIBAL
CIRCUIT GROUP**

MASTER KEYNOTE:
SUPPORT

The *Ego Circuit* and the
Defence Circuit

The three circuit groups divide all human interaction into fundamental principles:
Individuals are interested in themselves, *Collective People* are interested in humanity as a whole and *Tribal People* are interested in the family and the immediate community.
Individuals are acoustic, *Collective People* are visual and *Tribal People* are tactile.

Relationships between people with very different circuitry can therefore be very difficult. For example, in a couple where one person is Individual and another Tribal, the difficulty will always be that the Individual needs someone to listen to them whereas the Tribal Person simply needs to be touched.

Circuitry never lies, but neither can you change a person's inherent nature. Sometimes differences really are irreconcilable.

THE FOUR INTEGRATION CHANNELS

The *Integration Channels* are not in fact a circuit. They are the foundation of our biodiversity, representing the evolutionary force that separates us from our mammalian past. They are the channels that formed as humans first began to walk upright, thus they represent our transition from being a mammal to becoming *Homo Erectus*.

The Integration Channels are what make us selfish, therefore ensuring our individual survival. Selfishness is actually good for the genes, since if we didn't look after ourselves first, our species would soon die out.

People with definition in these channels are here to display self-love by putting themselves first. This is exemplified by: *I love myself* (10) and *I empower myself* (34) by *listening to my intuition* (57) in *the Now* (20).

THE INTEGRATION CHANNELS

MASTER KEYNOTE:
INDIVIDUATION -
THE DESCENT INTO FORM

VOICE:
I AM NOW (20)

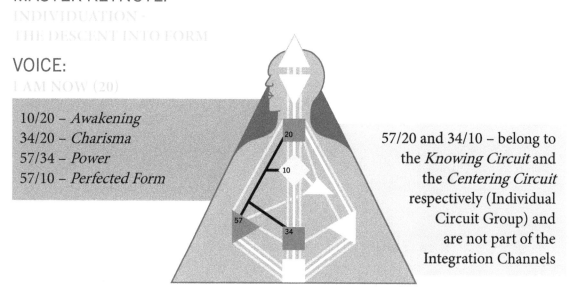

10/20 – *Awakening*
34/20 – *Charisma*
57/34 – *Power*
57/10 – *Perfected Form*

57/20 and 34/10 – belong to the *Knowing Circuit* and the *Centering Circuit* respectively (Individual Circuit Group) and are not part of the Integration Channels

The Integration Channels are resolutely separate from the six basic circuits in the bodygraph, and unlike them, they are not concerned with communication. Their self-absorbed and self-centred nature is very different from the Individual Channels in the Knowing and Centering Circuits. They are not at all concerned with how they impact others. They thrive by simply following their own path through life.

People with these channels often have an animal quality to them that is rooted in an ancient impulse for survival. The theme of their life has nothing to do with planning for the future or reflecting on the past. They are here to live in the Now. This is a survival instinct rooted in: "What was that noise over there? Am I safe? Will it eat me?"

As the most complex connective circuitry in Design, the Integration Channels give rise to a complexity of voices and potential action. They are after all, the only true existential voices we have.

Below are the various archetypal behaviour/awareness codes arising from these channels:

Gate Groups				The Voices of Individuation	Type
20				I Am Now	Mechanical
20	10			I Am Myself Now	Mechanical
20	10	57		I Know I Am Myself Now	Splenic
20	10	57	34	I Know I Am Myself in Action Now	Splenic
20	10		34	I Am Myself in Action Now	Mechanical
20		57	34	I Know I Am in Action Now	Splenic
20		57		I Know I Am Now	Splenic
20			34	I Am in Action Now	Mechanical

Individual Circuit Group
THE KNOWING CIRCUIT

MASTER KEYNOTE:
EMPOWERMENT

VOICES:
I AM NOW (20), I KNOW (23), I CAN (8), I ACT (12)

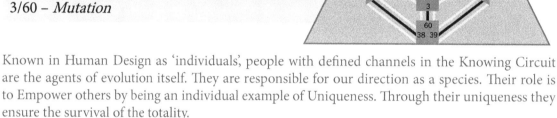

61/24 – *Awareness*
43/23 – *Structuring*
1/8 – *Inspiration*
2/14 – *The Beat*
3/60 – *Mutation*

39/55 – *Emoting*
22/12 – *Openness*
38/28 – *Struggle*
57/20 – *Brainwave*

Known in Human Design as 'individuals', people with defined channels in the Knowing Circuit are the agents of evolution itself. They are responsible for our direction as a species. Their role is to Empower others by being an individual example of Uniqueness. Through their uniqueness they ensure the survival of the totality.

The source of the Knowing Circuit is the channel 3/60 (Mutation), which is one of three channels known as the 'energy formats'. The theme of mutation is what drives the individual to be different from others. The purpose of mutation is to create constant change, giving birth to new forms in all walks of life. It is the driving force of evolution. Whereas 'integration' is about minding your own business, 'knowing' demands an audience in order that the mutation can bring change to the world.

The individual is here to Mutate (3/60) the Direction (2/14) of others as seen by Society (1/8). Individuals will always Provoke the spirit of others (39/55) by Fighting for what they value in life (38/28). Through their sharp Intuitive Awareness (57/20), flashes of Inspiration (61/24) and sudden Insight (43/23) what they say can have a lasting Impact on those who hear them (22/12).

Individuals don't like to be influenced or told what to do. They are inherently "deaf". They feel like outsiders in the world, and are often concerned about not fitting into society. They are in fact here to be different and are capable of intense genius, but never on demand. They have a tendency to melancholy, and at such times they can be at their most creative.

The life of the individual is always unpredictable. It is marked by alternating order and chaos, of times when they know and times when they do not know. They are the very source of creativity itself, and as agents of the creative process, they need to have a very deep acceptance of their nature to be comfortable in the world.

Individual Circuit Group
THE CENTERING CIRCUIT

MASTER KEYNOTE:
EMPOWERMENT

VOICES:
SACRAL SOUNDS

34/10 – *Exploration*
25/51 – *Initiation*

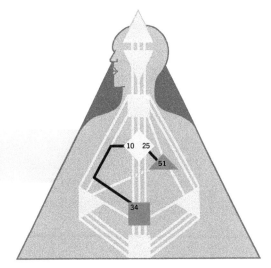

Although a minor circuit, the Centering Circuit has a huge impact on all other circuitry. Being focussed on Behaviour, it actually conditions others to behave differently from the way they normally would. The 34/10 Empowers others to follow their Convictions, while the 25/51 creates a deep sense of Competitiveness in those who meet it. However, Centering is not about changing the Behaviour of others. It is about Empowering others to love themselves and follow their own unique path in life.

Centering brings a great thrill of being oneself, as well as a deep love of life to individuality, which serves to enhance its power. To have the Power (34) to act according to one's Nature (10) and forge ahead with Courage (51) challenges and defines the Spirit of the Self (25). These people are always ready to 'leap into the void' just for the excitement of finding out what is on the other side. As with the Knowing Circuit, they are here to Empower others by following their own unique direction.

To be centred is to respond to life. Thus it demands surrender to a future that cannot be known or planned. To love oneself does not require awareness (there is no Awareness Centre in this circuit). It only requires a deep trust in the sacral response. People with a lot of activation in the Centering Circuit are classed as 'individuals', and they often feel like outsiders in society.

In spite of the resistance they may meet from others, they need great courage to follow their own convictions in life. Theirs is a life of self-empowerment which in turn also empowers others to love themselves. If they cannot have an impact on others, these people can end up feeling deeply melancholic and lonely in the world.

Collective Circuit Group
THE UNDERSTANDING CIRCUIT

MASTER KEYNOTE:
SHARING

VOICES:
I EXPERIMENT (16), I THINK (62), I LEAD (31)

63/4 – *Exploration*	9/52 – *Concentration*
17/62 – *Acceptance*	18/58 – *Judgement*
7/31 – *Alpha*	48/16 – *Wavelength*
5/15 – *Rhythm*	

This circuit is about being Focused and Concentrated (its format energy is the 9/52 Channel of Concentration), in order to understand the Patterns of Life (5). Once a pattern has been found, it has to be tested through Experimentation (16), improved through Correction (18), resolved through Depth (48) and grounded through Opinion (17). Once the Formula (4) underlying the pattern has been verified, only then can it be seen as reliable and used to project into the future. This is essentially a forward-looking circuit, which projects its patterns into the future in order to lead, in contrast to the Sensing Circuit, which reflects on the past in order to remember.

The keynote here is Sharing, so this is an inherently social group. The patterns that are being understood are passed on to others for the benefit of the Collective. These are very logical people, often serious, and they may love to argue a point. They can also be very opinionated. The secret of Logic is repetition. Logical people are here to repeat something over and over until they master it. They are detail-oriented, sceptical and doubtful, with an insatiable need for answers. However, these people by design are usually never satisfied with their answers, since they are driven by the interminable need to question and challenge. This is after all, the foundation of scientific thought. The constant need to focus on improvement means that these people can become extremely talented in any field of endeavour.

Logical people are very insecure without a natural sense of rhythm in their life. They are cool-headed and often have a very particular sense of taste. They are often desperate for recognition in order that they can be of service. Unlike all the other major circuits, the Understanding Circuit does not have direct access to energy (there is no motor defined directly to the Throat Centre). The implication of this is that logical people are always seeking energy (often in the form of funding) from others in order to work cooperatively. They are the natural leaders of society because of their gift of reading the patterns and trends of the future, and because of their ability to see things from a non-emotional perspective.

Collective Circuit Group
THE SENSING CIRCUIT

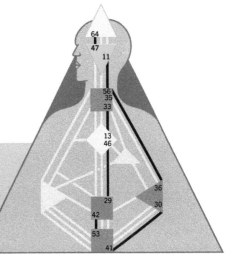

MASTER KEYNOTE:
SHARING

VOICES:
I REMEMBER (33), I BELIEVE (56), I FEEL (35)

64/47 – *Abstraction*	53/42 – *Maturation*
11/56 – *Curiosity*	41/30 – *Recognition*
13/33 – *The Prodigal*	35/36 – *Transitoriness*
29/46 – *Discovery*	

This circuit is about Experiencing and Reflecting on experience in order to learn. The format energy (53/42) represents the Spiral of Life and is about Cycles – beginnings and endings.
The theme of the Sensing Circuit is 'change through crisis' (35/36). It is not about success or failure, but Discovery (29/46). The Revelations in this circuit only come at the end of the experience, upon Reflection (13/33).

Like the Understanding Circuit, the keynote here is Sharing. Experiences, feelings, emotions and reflections are all ultimately for the benefit of the Collective. This is about learning from the past. When people connect to each other within this circuit they share their reflections. There is no purpose to this circuitry other than experience itself.

There is no splenic awareness in this circuit, which is ruled by the emotional wave of hope and pain. Thus the greatest lesson for people with definition in this circuit is patience. Where the Solar Plexus Centre is concerned, clarity can only come over time. These people are vulnerable and potentially unhealthy if they enter into situations wrongly or carrying an expectation. Since this circuit is about experience rather than goals, anyone with definition in this circuit needs to have a good sense of humour and perspective. If a situation turns out differently than one expected, that is never a failure, but a discovery.

Since this circuit is driven by desire for change, these people are often being caught in their own expectations based on a philosophy of: "if I do this, I'll get that". This circuitry brings a certain restlessness and sense of boredom with things that do not bring change. Because this also translates into sexuality, there are more broken marriages and disappointments because of this circuitry than any other. The trick for such people is to understand that they cannot make sense out of life as it is happening, but that they are literally genetically programmed to be a growing repository of wisdom and experience rather than what they perceive as successful.

Tribal Circuit Group
THE EGO CIRCUIT

MASTER KEYNOTE:
SUPPORT

VOICES:
I HAVE (45)

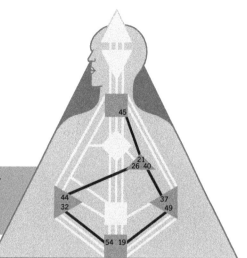

54/32 – *Transformation*	37/40 – *Community*
44/26 – *Surrender*	21/45 – *Money Line*
19/49 – *Synthesis*	

This circuit, representing the Tribe (community) and its Laws, is the bedrock of human society, being the foundation upon which our way of life is structured and maintained. It is the circuit of the Mundane Plane and the Material World.

The role of the tribe is twofold: to Transform individual ambition (54/32) into successful Teamwork (44/26) that ensures continued Protection and Control (21/45); and to build balanced Relationships (19/49) that support and nurture each person's place in the Community (37/40). It's not about direction (there is no G-Centre), neither is it mental nor philosophical (there is no Ajna Centre). It's focused exclusively on maintaining the well-being and growth of the Community. Coming together in the Tribe involves individual sacrifice.

Unlike the other major circuits, which focus on the Throat Centre, this circuit centres around the Ego Centre, our 'tribal heart'. This tribal heart is a communal heart, rather than the individual emotional heart.

These people are always trying to find a balance between work and rest. They need to work and be well valued for the work they do. They are usually happiest working in groups. Wherever you see this circuitry, there is always a bargain to be made. These are people who need to place a material value on themselves and whatever they have to offer. This is the philosophy of: 'you scratch my back and I'll scratch yours'. These are 'salt of the earth people' who need community and family. Their greatest concern is having enough food, money or affection.

The Ego Circuit is centred around the senses of touch and smell. These are people who need to shake your hand or hug you in order to know who you are. They need to meet you up close so that they can 'smell' if you belong in their 'tribe'. Metaphorically speaking, they don't trust anything unless they can smell it.

Tribal Circuit Group
THE DEFENCE CIRCUIT

MASTER KEYNOTE:
SUPPORT

VOICES:
SACRAL SOUNDS

59/6 – *Mating*
27/50 – *Preservation*

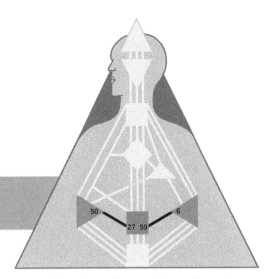

As the second of the two minor circuits, this is the circuit of our Sexuality and has a huge impact on all other circuitry. Just as the Centering Circuit empowers people to be unique and separate, the Defence Circuit pulls people into the heart of the Community. These people have the power to bring even the most stringent individuals, i.e. outsiders, into the Community.

The role of the Defence Circuit is to establish Values that support the Genetic Continuity of the tribe or family and offer Nurture and Care in order that its Offspring can Mature to adulthood, (27/50) thereby Fostering Children who will in turn Produce more Children (59/6). This reproduction ensures that our species can continue.

When you bring together the Defence and the Ego Circuits what emerges is the basis of the human life process. There is no survival for the young without the protection and nourishment of the community (shelter, food, education). The material plane exists only to serve these demands.

PART 2

CHANNELS AND GATES

The 'meat' of the Bodygraph is made up of the 36 Channels and the 64 Gates. When we first come to study Human Design, we tend to want instant answers about what each gate and channel means. However, the longer one studies Human Design, the deeper the labyrinth seems to go. Every channel and gate has many layers of keynotes associated with it, and each contributes to its meaning and function.

Added to this, gates and channels cannot be taken alone, but have to be understood in relation to each other. This is really the job of a professional analyst, who is trained to synthesise all the layers of knowledge contained in the bodygraph into simple and practical formulas.

Below are listed all the channels and gates, as well as their main keynotes. Below each gate and channel you will also find short descriptions, which are simplifications of the way in which they function. The Advanced Keynotes are drawn from many tributaries of Human Design knowledge, giving an overview of the many different layers and themes that make up each gate.

The descriptions below are based on the activity of gates and channels that are already defined, rather than in undefined centres. The behaviour of gates when they are in undefined centres, known as dormant gates, is beyond the scope of this current book.

It is important to realise that every gate has six line activations which add a further nuance to its functioning. Added to this, there are distinct differences in the functioning of conscious and unconscious gates as well as authentic behaviour patterns, not-self behaviour patterns and planetary influences. Students of Human Design should therefore always be wary of generalising about the functioning of channels and gates. You may for example, have a very social channel activated in your design, but it may be activated by only first lines, which means that you may be interested in social behaviour without being in the least bit social yourself!

Perhaps the best advice for anyone wanting to understand the gates and channels is to watch them in real life in the people around you. You can use these keynotes to help you see how the gates and channels actually operate in the world.

HOW TO USE 'PART 2' OF THIS BOOK

CIRCUIT:

Each channel forms a part of a wider 'circuit' or collection of channels. For further information refer to Part 1 on circuits.

QUICK REFERENCE THEME:

Brief yet practical summaries of each channel and gate. These themes generally refer to gates and channels that are in DEFINED centres, rather than in undefined centres.

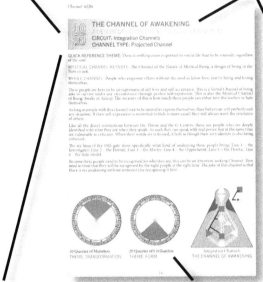

COLOUR SCHEME:

Each page is colour coded according to its circuit group –

BROWN – Integration Channels
GREEN – Individual Circuit Group
BLUE – Collective Circuit Group
ORANGE – Tribal Circuit Group

QUARTER:

Every gate or hexagram belongs to one of 4 quarters in the Human Design Wheel. Depending on which quarter the gate is from, it has an underlying fulfilment through that theme.

The 4 possible spheres of fulfilment are: Transformation, Relationships, Mind and Form.

ADVANCED KEYNOTES:

For those who wish to see the many other hidden layers beneath a single gate.

These are additional keynotes taken from a wide range of related Human Design sciences.

CHANNEL TYPE:

There are 4 types of channels –

MANIFESTING CHANNELS

Any channel that directly connects one of two motors (Solar Plexus, Heart/Ego) to the Throat Centre. Such channels share many common traits with manifestors, one example being an underlying theme of anger.

MANIFESTING GENERATED CHANNELS

The channel 34/20, is the only channel that directly connects with the Sacral Centre to the Throat Centre. This channel shares many common traits with manifesting generators, one example being a theme of impatience.

GENERATED CHANNELS

Any channel that defines the Sacral Centre (other than the 34/20). These channels share many common traits with Generators, one example being an underlying theme of frustration.

PROJECTED CHANNELS

Any channel that doesn't link one of three motors (the Sacral, Heart/Ego, Solar Plexus) directly to the Throat Centre. Such channels share many common traits with Projectors, one example being an undercurrent of resentment if not given the correct recognition.

THE CHANNEL OF AWAKENING
A DESIGN OF COMMITMENT TO HIGHER PRINCIPLES

10
20

CIRCUIT: Integration Channels
CHANNEL TYPE: Projected Channel

QUICK REFERENCE THEME: There is nothing more important to you in life than to be yourself, regardless of the cost.

MYSTICAL CHANNEL KEYNOTE: The Channel of the Nature of Mystical Being, a design of being in the Now or not.

WHOLE CHANNEL: People who empower others without the need to know how, just by being and loving themselves.

These people are here to be an expression of self-love and self-acceptance. This is a Verbal Channel of being able to survive under any circumstance through perfect self-expression. This is also the Mystical Channel of Being Awake or Asleep. The measure of this is how much these people can either love themselves or hate themselves.

As long as people with this channel wait to be invited to express themselves, their behaviour will perfectly suit any situation. If their self-expression is uninvited (which is more usual) they will always meet the resistance of others.

Like all the direct connections between the Throat and the G Centres, these are people who are deeply identified with what they say when they speak. As such they can speak with real power, but at the same time are vulnerable to criticism. When their words are criticised, it feels as though their very identity is also being criticised.

The six lines of the 10th gate show specifically what kind of awakening these people bring: Line 1 – the Investigator, Line 2 – the Hermit, Line 3 – the Martyr, Line 4 – the Opportunist, Line 5 – the Heretic, Line 6 – the Role Model.

Because these people need to be recognised for who they are, this can be an Attention-seeking Channel. They need to trust that they will be recognised by the right people at the right time. The joke of this channel is that there is no awakening without someone else recognising it first.

10 Quarter of Mutation
THEME: TRANSFORMATION

20 Quarter of Civilisation
THEME: FORM

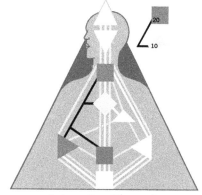

Integration Channels
THE CHANNEL OF AWAKENING

THE GATE OF BEHAVIOUR OF THE SELF – TREADING

QUICK REFERENCE THEME: People whose lives are an expression of their own uniqueness – The Love of Oneself.

DESCRIPTION: One of the Gates of Love, this gate is about the love of being oneself. When the 10 is connected to the 20 it has the means of expressing itself verbally and spontaneously (but not necessarily with awareness).

These people are here to express one of six behaviour patterns, according to which 10th gate line they have: the Investigator (1), the Hermit (2), the Martyr (3), the Opportunist (4), the Heretic (5) and the Role Model (6).

When the gate is not part of a defined channel, these people are often deeply concerned about the behaviour of others.

ADVANCED KEYNOTES

Primary Role Gate – The 6 behavioural roles
Gate of the Vessel of Love – The love of being oneself – The lip of the vessel, through which life pours
Foundation of Hexagram – 10.1 – Modesty
Personality Sun Crosses – Vessel of Love, Behaviour, Prevention
Genetic Codon Group – Arginine (25,17,21,51,38,10)

Gate of Melancholy – Melancholy that no one else knows how to behave
Mystical Gate – 'The Li' – The love of the Way
Gate of Sexuality (Caring) – Self Love or not
Design of Forms – Love as Form and Beauty (plants)
Other Keynotes – The Chameleon, The Winter Solstice

THE GATE OF THE NOW – CONTEMPLATION

QUICK REFERENCE THEME: People who are can only see life in the present moment. Everything has to be Now.

DESCRIPTION: The Gate of the "Now". These people are here to be totally absorbed in the present moment.

When connected to the 10 it expresses 'who we are' according to the line number of the 10. If not connected to a motor, the 20th is a verbal gate rather than an action gate. Such people cannot preempt what they are going to say before they say it. These are words or actions that simply bubble out in the moment.

ADVANCED KEYNOTES

Existential Expression Gate – Clarity/Action that can be instantaneous
Voice – I am Now
Foundation of Hexagram – 20.1 – Superficiality
Personality Sun Crosses – Sleeping Phoenix, The Now, Duality
Genetic Codon Group – Leucine (42,3,27,24,23,20)
Gate of Melancholy – Discomfort with the world as it is now

Dreamrave Key – Sight (Light Field)
Mystical Gate – The Existential Manifestation of the Way
Gate of Sexuality (Caring) – Gate of Individualism – Caring for Oneself or not
Design of Forms – The power to individuate/ The Hum (insects)
Other Keynotes – The Eternal Now

34/20 THE CHANNEL OF CHARISMA
A DESIGN WHERE THOUGHTS MUST BECOME DEEDS

CIRCUIT: Integration Channels
CHANNEL TYPE: Manifesting Generated Channel

QUICK REFERENCE THEME: The healthiest thing for you is to be continually busy in life, but it is essential that you are busy doing something that you love.

MYSTICAL CHANNEL KEYNOTE: The Channel of the Nature of Mystical Being, a design of being in the Now or not.

WHOLE CHANNEL: People who are generally unavailable to the outside world on account of being absorbed in constant activity from one moment to the next.

These people have a deep need to be busy and involved in activity. True charisma comes when they are busy doing things they love. When they are involved in activity that they love, they naturally empower others with their charisma.

These are often people who 'can't sit down'. Without the 57, they are usually not even aware that they are so busy. The keynote to this channel is 'a design where Thoughts must become Deeds', which means that they usually end up acting out their thoughts with disastrous consequences. However, as long as they are responding to life rather than trying to follow their mind, they will always be busy with the correct things, which will in turn always keep them healthy.

Without the presence of the 57, this is power that can always erupt explosively and spontaneously and without awareness.

Technically people with this channel are Manifestors. However, their strategy is that of a Generator. It is very difficult for them to wait because of their constant need to be in motion. They are people who need subtle guidance from others in order that they can respond correctly. The best guides for them are those with the channel 43/23. However, these people can never be told what to do by someone else. They are stringent individuals.

34 Quarter of Mutation
THEME: TRANSFORMATION

20 Quarter of Civilisation
THEME: FORM

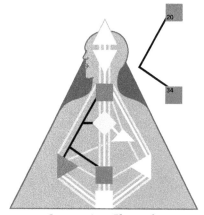

Integration Channels
THE CHANNEL OF CHARISMA

34 THE GATE OF POWER — THE POWER OF THE GREAT

QUICK REFERENCE THEME: People whose actions are generally independent and self-centred, but who do not need to feel guilty about the fact.

DESCRIPTION: This is a gate of pure vital energy that emerges naturally out of response to external stimuli. It is a Gate of Self-empowerment; through the intuition (when connected to the 57), through behaviour (when connected to the 10) and through activity (when connected to the 20).

This gate is rooted in the urge to display how different one is from others. It fuels the survival of the individual and is the only Asexual Gate coming from the sacral. Unlike all the other gates of the sacral, this is the only Gate of being Unavailable. This manifests as someone being unavailable because they are busy (when connected to the 34), unavailable because they are following their own convictions (when connected to the 10) or unavailable to listen (when connected to the 57).

Without the 57, the 34 is a power that is unaware of itself and therefore can potentially be dangerous to itself or others.

ADVANCED KEYNOTES

Energy Display Gate – Self-empowerment, independence
Foundation of Hexagram – 34.1 – The Bully
Genetic Codon Group – Asparagine (34,43)
Gate of Sexuality (Caring) – Gate of Individuation (unavailable for caring)

Gate of Melancholy – Frustration at not being able to use one's power in the Now
Design of Forms – The power to proliferate (birds, reptiles, fish)
Other Keynotes – Unavailable through being Self-absorbed

20 THE GATE OF THE NOW — CONTEMPLATION

QUICK REFERENCE THEME: People who can only see life in the present moment. Everything has to be Now.

DESCRIPTION: The Gate of the "Now". These people are here to be totally absorbed in the present moment.

When connected to the 10 it expresses 'who we are' according the line number of the 10. If not connected to a motor, the 20th is a verbal gate rather than an action gate. Such people cannot preempt what they are going to say before they say it. These are words or actions that simply bubble out in the moment.

ADVANCED KEYNOTES

Existential Expression Gate – Clarity/Action that can be instantaneous
Voice – I am Now
Foundation of Hexagram – 20.1 – Superficiality
Personality Sun Crosses – Sleeping Phoenix, The Now, Duality
Genetic Codon Group – Leucine (42,3,27,24,23,20)
Gate of Melancholy – Discomfort with the world as it is now

Dreamrave Key – Sight (Light Field)
Mystical Gate – The Existential Manifestation of the Way
Gate of Sexuality (Caring) – Gate of Individualism – Caring for Oneself or not
Design of Forms – The power to individuate/ The Hum (insects)
Other Keynotes – The Eternal Now

THE CHANNEL OF POWER
A DESIGN OF AN ARCHETYPE

CIRCUIT: Integration Channels
CHANNEL TYPE: Generated Channel

QUICK REFERENCE THEME: Your body has a very acute early warning system that is constantly attuned to your immediate environment. When you can learn to consistently trust in your intuition, you will become an archetype of true power.

WHOLE CHANNEL: People whose intuitive awareness keeps them healthy through constant response.

These people have to allow their body to respond in the now. Only when they learn to trust in their moment-to-moment response will they be free from their fear of the unknown. This channel represents a consistently operating intuition and in this respect it is very different for example, from the sporadic flashes of intuition of the 57/20.

These people are constantly on guard and alert. They always have to trust the animal within them. They are always ready to jump either into battle or out of the way of danger in a split second. Their animal energy is purely based on their attunement to sound and vibration. For example, they will always hear exactly what is really being said through the tone of the speaker, rather than through the words themselves.

The power of this channel is only seen through spontaneous response, before either the emotions or the mind comes into play. It is the pure essence of survival. Sometimes these people can appear very cool to outsiders, but when responding naturally to life they truly represent the archetype of what it means to be a true human being.

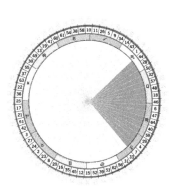

57 Quarter of Duality
THEME: RELATIONSHIPS

34 Quarter of Mutation
THEME: TRANSFORMATION

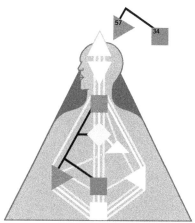

Integration Channels
THE CHANNEL OF POWER

THE GATE OF INTUITIVE CLARITY – THE GENTLE

QUICK REFERENCE THEME: People whose intuitive awareness always ensures their survival.

DESCRIPTION: This is the Gate of the Right Ear and of Hearing in the Now. This gate is the source of all mammalian awareness, representing our deepest intuitions, which are here to guide us towards survival and well-being.

If you have the 57 as part of a definition, you have a very acute attunement to both vibration and sound. This gate is literally where we hear from our immune system. It is also the Gate of Fear of the Unknown (the future). It needs the raw responsive power of the 34 to ensure it is safe, since awareness on its own can do nothing. Without the presence of the 34, the body is powerless to react.

As individuals, these people are designed not to be influenced by others – thus they have selective hearing. If they remain focused intently in the moment, they can always eliminate their underlying fear of the future and the unknown.

ADVANCED KEYNOTES

Splenic Awareness Gate – The right ear (existential) that hears the truth in the Now
Foundation of Hexagram – 57.1 – Confusion
Personality Sun Crosses – Penetration, Intuition, Clarion
Genetic Codon Group – Alanine (57,48,18,46)
Awareness Stream – Stream of Intuition (Possibility of Intuitive Clarity)
Gate of Sexuality (Caring) – A design of Concern/Self-concern

Dreamrave Key – Attunement (Light Field)
Gate of Fear – The Fear of the Future/the Unexpected
Gate of Melancholy – Melancholy through hearing
Design of Forms – The Ears (mammals)/Vibration awareness (insects)/Vibration attunement (plants)/Acoustic clarity
Physiology – The lymphatic brain
Other Keynotes – Gate of Hearing through the Body, The Hunch

THE GATE OF POWER – THE POWER OF THE GREAT

QUICK REFERENCE THEME: People whose actions are generally independent and self-centred, but who do not need to feel guilty about the fact.

DESCRIPTION: This is a gate of pure vital energy that emerges naturally out of response to external stimuli. It is a Gate of Self-empowerment; through the intuition (when connected to the 57), through behaviour (when connected to the 10) and through activity (when connected to the 20).

This gate is rooted in the urge to display how different one is from others. It fuels the survival of the individual and is the only Asexual Gate coming from the sacral. Unlike all the other gates of the sacral, this is the only Gate of being Unavailable. This manifests as someone being unavailable because they are busy (when connected to the 34), unavailable because they are following their own convictions (when connected to the 10) or unavailable to listen (when connected to the 57).

Without the 57, the 34 is a power that is unaware of itself and therefore can potentially be dangerous to itself or others.

ADVANCED KEYNOTES

Energy Display Gate – Self-empowerment, independence
Foundation of Hexagram – 34.1 – The Bully
Genetic Codon Group – Asparagine (34,43)
Gate of Sexuality (Caring) – Gate of Individuation (unavailable for caring)

Gate of Melancholy – Frustration at not being able to use one's power in the Now
Design of Forms – The power to proliferate (birds, reptiles, fish)
Other Keynotes – Unavailable through being Self-absorbed

57 / 10 THE CHANNEL OF PERFECTED FORM
A DESIGN OF SURVIVAL

CIRCUIT: Integration Channels
CHANNEL TYPE: Generated Channel

QUICK REFERENCE THEME: Your life is a canvas and your behaviour is your art. If you follow your intuition you will always create beauty through your actions.

SEXUALITY KEYNOTE: The Channel of Response-ability.

WHOLE CHANNEL: People whose behaviour is guided by their intuition, also known as the Channel of Beauty.

Being the Creative Channel of the Integration System, the theme of this channel is the "art" of survival. When the 10th Gate of Behaviour is linked to the 57th Gate of Intuition, survival of the individual is guaranteed.

These people need to perfect their form, whatever that form means for them. They are here to create something beautiful out of their lives (many designers and architects have this channel). They are here to love the art of creating simply for their own enjoyment. They often cannot survive without creating some kind of beauty around them.

These people have a clarity that cuts right through their feelings and thoughts, and a rare ability to 'think on their feet'. When they follow their intuition, their behavioural strategy naturally manifests beauty.

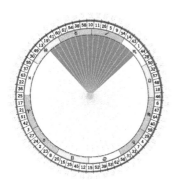
57 Quarter of Duality
THEME: RELATIONSHIPS

10 Quarter of Mutation
THEME: TRANSFORMATION

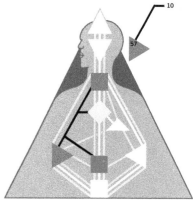
Integration Channels
THE CHANNEL OF PERFECTED FORM

57 THE GATE OF INTUITIVE CLARITY – THE GENTLE

QUICK REFERENCE THEME: People whose intuitive awareness always ensures their survival.

DESCRIPTION: This is the Gate of the Right Ear and of Hearing in the Now. This gate is the source of all mammalian awareness, representing our deepest intuitions, which are here to guide us towards survival and well-being.

If you have the 57 as part of a definition, you have a very acute attunement to both vibration and sound. This gate is literally where we hear from our immune system. It is also the Gate of Fear of the Unknown (the future). It needs the raw responsive power of the 34 to ensure it is safe, since awareness on its own can do nothing. Without the presence of the 34, the body is powerless to react.

As individuals, these people are designed not to be influenced by others – thus they have selective hearing. If they remain focused intently in the moment, they can always eliminate their underlying fear of the future and the unknown.

ADVANCED KEYNOTES

Splenic Awareness Gate – The right ear (existential) that hears the truth in the Now
Foundation of Hexagram – 57.1 – Confusion
Personality Sun Crosses – Penetration, Intuition, Clarion
Genetic Codon Group – Alanine (57,48,18,46)
Awareness Stream – Stream of Intuition (Possibility of Intuitive Clarity)
Gate of Sexuality (Caring) – A design of Concern/ Self-concern

Dreamrave Key – Attunement (Light Field)
Gate of Fear – The Fear of the Future/the Unexpected
Gate of Melancholy – Melancholy through hearing
Design of Forms – The Ears (mammals)/Vibration awareness (insects)/Vibration attunement (plants)/ Acoustic clarity
Physiology – The lymphatic brain
Other Keynotes – Gate of Hearing through the Body, The Hunch

10 THE GATE OF BEHAVIOUR OF THE SELF – TREADING

QUICK REFERENCE THEME: People whose lives are an expression of their own uniqueness – The Love of Oneself.

DESCRIPTION: One of the Gates of Love, this gate is about the love of being oneself. When the 10 is connected to the 20 it has the means of expressing itself verbally and spontaneously (but not necessarily with awareness).

These people are here to express one of six behaviour patterns, according to which 10th gate line they have: the Investigator (1), the Hermit (2), the Martyr (3), the Opportunist (4), the Heretic (5) and the Role Model (6).

When the gate is not part of a defined channel, these people are often deeply concerned about the behaviour of others.

ADVANCED KEYNOTES

Primary Role Gate – The 6 behavioural roles
Gate of the Vessel of Love – The love of being oneself – The lip of the vessel, through which life pours
Foundation of Hexagram – 10.1 – Modesty
Personality Sun Crosses – Vessel of Love, Behaviour, Prevention
Genetic Codon Group – Arginine (25,17,21,51,38,10)

Gate of Melancholy – Melancholy that no one else knows how to behave
Mystical Gate – 'The Li' – The love of the Way
Gate of Sexuality (Caring) – Self Love or not
Design of Forms – Love as Form and Beauty (plants)
Other Keynotes – The Chameleon, The Winter Solstice

THE CHANNEL OF AWARENESS
A DESIGN OF A THINKER
CIRCUIT: The Knowing Circuit
CHANNEL TYPE: Projected Channel

QUICK REFERENCE THEME: So long as you are not using it to try and resolve your own life, your mind is always capable of inspiring someone else to see life in a totally new light.

WHOLE CHANNEL: The world's great thinkers. These people are here to inspire others to think about life's mysteries. These are minds that constantly need to explore new intellectual areas in new ways. Such minds are capable of creating whole new ways of thinking about things, and they need a great deal of recognition in this.

These are people who need and love silence. They can be the kind of people who experience sounds or voices inside their heads. Because they are acoustically oriented, listening to or playing music can be an extremely soothing way for them to release their mental pressure.

These are melancholic minds where inspiration comes suddenly and unexpectedly, but can never be controlled or predicted.

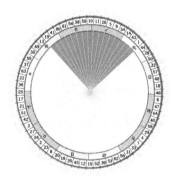

61 Quarter of Mutation
THEME: TRANSFORMATION

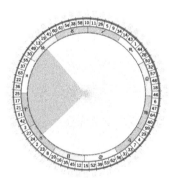

24 Quarter of Initiation
THEME: MIND

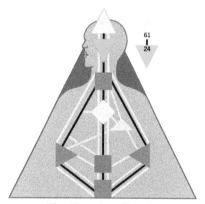

The Knowing Circuit:
THE CHANNEL OF AWARENESS

THE GATE OF MYSTERY — INNER TRUTH

QUICK REFERENCE THEME: People who are under considerable mental pressure to resolve what is unknown.

DESCRIPTION: As the Gate of Inner Truth, this is the place where inspiration can potentially be mutative. In other words, of the many thoughts and inspirations that come flooding through this gate, some may have a lasting impact on the lives of others. Such inspirations are often experienced as the 'light-bulb going on in the brain', or as sudden moments of epiphany or 'satori'. This can be deeply inspiring for others as long as it can be expressed clearly and at the right moment. The 61 puts the 24 under pressure to come up with a concept that must eventually be expressed. Without the 24, the 61 is the love of a mystery without the need of solving it.

These people are great thinkers and musers who love to delve into the unknown, but can never solve their own life through thinking. They must accept that some things are unknowable, and they need to learn to let go of rationalising and controlling their own thoughts. As a source of potential mutation, their mind is beyond their own understanding, and if they do not follow the true authority in their design (which can never be their mind), they will very likely become deeply melancholic about their lives.

ADVANCED KEYNOTES

Pressure Gate – The pressure to know something totally new/the pressure to rationalise
Foundation of Hexagram – 61.1 – Occult Knowledge
Personality Sun Crosses – Maya, Thinking, Obscuration

Genetic Codon Group – Isoleucine (60,61,16)
Awareness Stream – Stream of Knowing (Fuel of Mystery)
Gate of Melancholy – Melancholy over lack of inspiration
Other Keynotes – Gate of Madness and Dreaming (61,63,64)

 # THE GATE OF RATIONALISATION — THE RETURN

QUICK REFERENCE THEME: People who go over and over things seeking to rationalise them.

DESCRIPTION: This gate screens all the new thoughts that come through the 61, selecting what is useful and potentially inspiring for others. It has great potential to impact others once it is clear. Without the 61, these are people looking for a mystery to resolve. If they are not clear about their own nature, their mind can become their own worst enemy, constantly reviewing their own life and trying to make decisions for them.

These are very single-minded, individual thinkers who need considerable time to contemplate before the penny drops (as in the 43). They have a great need to hear things over and over before they are integrated and make sense. These are also the kind of people who will not let go of a worry until it is resolved. Resolutions usually come when they can find an atmosphere of silence (often in the middle of the night!).

ADVANCED KEYNOTES

Conceptual Processing Gate – The struggle to resolve a thought process
Foundation of Hexagram – 24.1 – The sin of omission
Personality Sun Crosses – Four Ways, Rationalisation, Incarnation
Genetic Codon Group – Leucine (42,3,27,24,20,23)
Awareness Stream – Stream of Knowing (Potential to Rationalise)

Gate of Fear – The Fear of Ignorance
Gate of Anxiety – Anxiety over Mysteries
Gate of Melancholy – Melancholy over no resolution and therefore no inner silence
Other Keynotes – Gate of Migraines, Silence, Mantras, Pondering

THE CHANNEL OF STRUCTURING
A DESIGN OF INDIVIDUALITY (GENIUS TO FREAK)
CIRCUIT: The Knowing Circuit
CHANNEL TYPE: Projected Channel

QUICK REFERENCE THEME: If you cannot explain your insights clearly, you will always drive people away. If you learn the right timing for when to speak and when not to speak, you will always get the recognition you deserve.

WHOLE CHANNEL: These people are here to impact the way others see things. At their best they can totally change the way we think about something. They have a real capability for innovative thinking that is based on improving the efficiency of how energy is used. This is not about gradual improvement and modification of existing functions, but thinking that can bring quantum leaps. In organisations, they always have the capacity to bring higher levels of efficiency.

The other side of these people is that they can also be "blurters" and often go through life feeling they are not really being heard. It is essential for them to learn to control the timing of when they speak or they will alienate themselves from others. Ideally, this channel operates at its best when it waits to be invited to speak.

These are people who have a deep need to talk things through with others in order that they can hear what they know (it often comes as a surprise to them). Furthermore, when the channel is unconscious (coloured red), this is a voice that speaks without knowing what it's saying. This can either be a great gift or it can lead to great misunderstandings.

As children, these are people who need to be constantly encouraged to explain their thinking. If they learn how to do this when young, it can save a lot of difficulty later in life.

43 Quarter of Mutation
THEME: TRANSFORMATION

23 Quarter of Civilisation
THEME: FORM

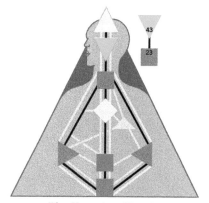

The Knowing Circuit:
THE CHANNEL OF STRUCTURING

THE GATE OF INSIGHT – BREAKTHROUGH

QUICK REFERENCE THEME: People who have a real gift for expressing their thoughts in a novel and creative way.

DESCRIPTION: This gate transforms the rationalised truths of the 24 into unique perspectives that are ready to be converted into speech codes in the 23. These are people who have a unique "inner voice" which is always going through the process of structuring its knowing. They always have to learn to wait for the penny to drop before they can make themselves heard. These are minds that only know what they are interested in and are not necessarily interested in what others know.

It is very difficult to teach these people anything as they have to know everything for themselves. Added to this, the 43 is a Gate of Deafness, which means that they are designed to block out the knowing of others until they can see something in their own way.

As part of individual circuitry, the insights that come through this gate move as a pulse from knowing to not knowing. Without the 23, the dilemma of this gate is always how to translate the knowing into language.

ADVANCED KEYNOTES

Conceptual Crystallisation Gate – Spontaneous resolution of a concept (the voice of the Muse, the inner ear)
Foundation of Hexagram – 43.1 – Patience
Personality Sun Crosses – Explanation, Insight, Dedication
Genetic Codon Group – Asparagine (43,34)
Awareness Stream – Stream of Knowing (Possibility of Insight)

Gate of Fear – The Fear of Rejection
Gate of Anxiety – Anxiety over Assimilation
Gate of Melancholy – Melancholy over inefficiency
Other Keynotes – Gate of Efficiency, Gate of Deafness (38,39,43), The Muse

 # THE GATE OF ASSIMILATION – SPLITTING APART

QUICK REFERENCE THEME: People whose recognition depends entirely upon the timing of when they speak and their use of language.

DESCRIPTION: This gate represents the potential ability to put language around the concepts that come out of the 43. The purpose of this gate is to express individual insights that inject new and innovative ways of thinking into society.

These people are often misunderstood and treated as outsiders, hence the Channel Keynote – 'Genius to Freak'. Their expression can be totally out of place and socially inappropriate. They must learn to eliminate intolerance by waiting to be invited to share their knowing clearly.

ADVANCED KEYNOTES

Conceptual Expression Gate – Impulse to impart knowing or not
Voice – I know, I don't know
Foundation of Hexagram – 23.1 – Proselytisation
Personality Sun Crosses – Explanation, Assimilation, Dedication

Awareness Stream – Stream of Knowing (Expression of Assimilation)
Gate of Melancholy – Frustration over not being able to explain oneself clearly
Other Keynotes – Gate of Blurting, Genius to Freak

THE CHANNEL OF STRUGGLE
A DESIGN OF STUBBORNNESS
CIRCUIT: The Knowing Circuit
CHANNEL TYPE: Projected Channel

QUICK REFERENCE THEME: Your life is an archetypal hero's journey against overwhelming odds. The goal is to remain yourself and go your own way no matter what anyone else thinks or says.

SEXUALITY KEYNOTE: The Channel of Turmoil.

WHOLE CHANNEL: This is the "I did it my way" mentality. These people love a good fight and are here to hone themselves on life. They are also here to stand up for themselves, and consequently often have to do it alone. Because this is a Projected Channel, they need to have people in their lives that allow them to struggle. Theirs is a constant struggle between purpose and lack of purpose.

The struggle in this channel is deeply individual and is punctuated by unpredictable periods of melancholy. Their fear of time running out drives them to get as much out of life as possible. However, these individuals actually give direction to society and can be of enormous value in empowering others. Their great strength is their stubbornness – they will not give up on something that holds meaning for them.

Due to its connection to the spleen, this is a Health Channel. These people are always healthiest when pushing themselves, and they usually need to channel their fighting spirit into some form of enlivening, strenuous physical activity.

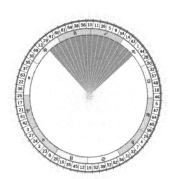

38 Quarter of Mutation
THEME: TRANSFORMATION

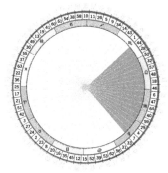

28 Quarter of Duality
THEME: RELATIONSHIPS

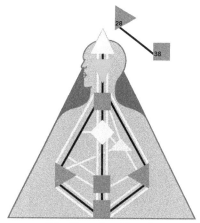

The Knowing Circuit
THE CHANNEL OF STRUGGLE

THE GATE OF THE FIGHTER — OPPOSITION

QUICK REFERENCE THEME: People who are at their best when up against odds. Natural born warriors.

DESCRIPTION: These are people that love a good fight, and are always ready to stand up for their independence. This is the pressure to fight against the odds in order to establish a sense of value and purpose in life. They need to feel a sense of carefreeness in their lives and consequently these people can feel very depressed if they are not doing something that gives them a sense of their life being of true value.

Since the 38 is one of the three Gates of Deafness (38,39,43), these people can be very stubborn as they are not here by design to be overly influenced by others. This deafness is in fact their protection from compromising their sense of purpose to outside pressure or influence.

Without the 28 these people need to be careful not to get locked into a fight with the wrong things or the wrong people and end up wasting their energy and health on something that they do not love. The 28 brings the awareness of what is actually worth fighting for.

ADVANCED KEYNOTES

Pressure Gate – The energy to struggle or not
Foundation of Hexagram – 38.1 – Qualification
Personality Sun Crosses – Tension, Opposition, Prevention
Genetic Codon Group – Arginine (10,38,25,17,21,51)
Awareness Stream – Stream of Intuition (Fuel to Fight for survival)

Gate of Sexuality (Caring) – Gate of Carelessness, a design of Incaution
Dreamrave Key – Aggression (Demon Realm)
Gate of Melancholy – Not knowing what to fight for
Design of Forms – Gate of Aggressiveness (mammals)
Other Keynotes – Gate of Deafness (38,39,43)

 # THE GATE OF THE GAME PLAYER — PREPONDERANCE OF THE GREAT

QUICK REFERENCE THEME: People who are always ready to take risks in order to find meaning in life.

DESCRIPTION: In this gate lies the potential of an individual to know spontaneously what is worth fighting for and what is not.

Driven by a fear of life running out (the Fear of Death) these people are ready to take any risk that makes them feel more alive. However, as long as they are listening to their intuition and following their strategy, there is no such thing as a risk for them. This is the Gate of the Need to find Purpose in One's Life.

Without the 38, these people may go simply flit from one thing to the next in a search for meaning. When the 38 is present, there is the possibility of digging one's heels in and finding meaning in one particular thing.

ADVANCED KEYNOTES

Awareness Processing Gate – To know what is worth fighting for
Foundation of Hexagram – 28.1 – Preparation
Personality Sun Crosses – Unexpected, Risks, Alignment
Genetic Codon Group – Aspartic Acid (28,32)
Awareness Stream – Stream of Intuition (Potential to survive through struggle)
Gate of Sexuality (Caring) – Gate of Carefreeness, a design of Uncertainty

Dreamrave Key – Fear (Demon Realm)
Gate of Melancholy – Life as devoid of purpose
Gate of Fear – The Fear of Death
Design of Forms – Listening Intensity – The Stalker (mammals)
Gate of Love – The Love of Life
Gate of Memory – The Stubbornness to Listen
Other Keynotes – The Gate of Playfulness, The Gambler

THE BRAINWAVE
A DESIGN OF PENETRATING AWARENESS

CIRCUIT: The Knowing Circuit
CHANNEL TYPE: Projected Channel

QUICK REFERENCE THEME: You bring an incredible gift into the world through the acuteness of your intuition. Just because you can see the truth more quickly than others does not mean that you are here to share it. Wait until you are asked.

WHOLE CHANNEL: This channel is here to ensure the survival of the individual who carries it. It is a spontaneous voice with incredibly sharp intuition that arises so fast that the brain cannot even comprehend it until afterwards (hence its name 'The Brainwave'). It is an electrical impulse-wave that begins in the lymphatic system and registers almost instantly in the brain. These people can intuitively adapt to any circumstance without thinking about how they do it. They are the world's greatest improvisers as long as they can overcome their fear of the unknown.

No matter how quickly they can intuit an answer, these people must wait to be invited to release their wisdom. If they blurt it out, they are usually vehemently resisted or deeply misunderstood.

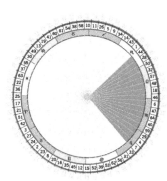

57 Quarter of Duality
THEME: RELATIONSHIPS

20 Quarter of Civilisation
THEME: FORM

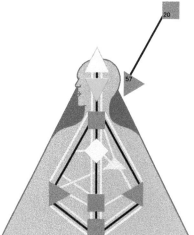

The Knowing Circuit
THE BRAINWAVE

THE GATE OF INTUITIVE CLARITY – THE GENTLE

QUICK REFERENCE THEME: People whose intuitive awareness always ensures their survival.

DESCRIPTION: This is the Gate of the Right Ear and of Hearing in the Now. This gate is the source of all mammalian awareness, representing our deepest intuitions, which are here to guide us towards survival and well-being.

If you have the 57 as part of a definition, you have a very acute attunement to both vibration and sound. This gate is literally where we hear from our immune system. It is also the Gate of Fear of the Unknown (the future). It needs the raw responsive power of the 34 to ensure it is safe, since awareness on its own can do nothing. Without the presence of the 34, the body is powerless to react. When connected to the 20, the awareness can always be expressed but not necessarily acted upon.

As individuals, these people are designed not to be influenced by others – thus they have selective hearing. If they remain focused intently in the moment, they can always eliminate their underlying fear of the future and the unknown.

ADVANCED KEYNOTES

Splenic Awareness Gate – The right ear (existential) that hears the truth in the Now
Foundation of Hexagram – 57.1 – Confusion
Personality Sun Crosses – Penetration, Intuition, Clarion
Genetic Codon Group – Alanine (57,48,18,46)
Awareness Stream – Stream of Intuition (Possibility of Intuitive Clarity)
Gate of Sexuality (Caring) – A design of Concern/Self-concern

Dreamrave Key – Attunement (Light Field)
Gate of Fear – The Fear of the Future/the Unexpected
Gate of Melancholy – Melancholy through hearing
Design of Forms – The Ears (mammals)/Vibration awareness (insects)/Vibration attunement (plants)/Acoustic clarity
Physiology – The lymphatic brain
Other Keynotes – Gate of Hearing through the Body, The Hunch

THE GATE OF THE NOW – CONTEMPLATION

QUICK REFERENCE THEME: People who can only see life in the present moment. Everything has to be Now.

DESCRIPTION: The Gate of the "Now". People whose awareness can only be transformed into action with the proper timing. It is not easy for such people to project themselves ahead into the future, since their power and clarity only emerges moment by moment. Without the 34, these are people who can always speak in the now, but cannot necessarily act on their words.

When not connected to a motor, the 20th is a verbal gate rather than an action gate within this channel. It expresses a totally individual knowing that can be as awesome and long as it is inappropriate.

ADVANCED KEYNOTES

Existential Expression Gate – Clarity/Action that can be instantaneous
Voice – I am Now
Foundation of Hexagram – 20.1 – Superficiality
Personality Sun Crosses – Sleeping Phoenix, The Now, Duality
Genetic Codon Group – Leucine (42,3,27,24,23,20)
Gate of Melancholy – Discomfort with the world as it is now

Dreamrave Key – Sight (Light Field)
Mystical Gate – The Existential Manifestation of The Way
Gate of Sexuality (Caring) – Gate of Individualism – Caring for Oneself or not
Design of Forms – The power to individuate/The Hum (insects)
Other Keynotes – The Eternal Now

THE CHANNEL OF EMOTING
A DESIGN OF MOODINESS
CIRCUIT: The Knowing Circuit
CHANNEL TYPE: Projected Channel

QUICK REFERENCE THEME: The secret to your life is to learn to appreciate the lows as much as you love the highs. When you can let go of wanting to control love, only then will you experience the freedom you seek.

SEXUALITY KEYNOTE: The Channel of Stimulation.

WHOLE CHANNEL: These people are here to embrace the lesson that life comes with both highs and lows, and to accept the endless cycles of sadness and joy. This is the Channel of Being Happy or Sad, of riding the emotional wave and tapping into the tremendous creativity that can come from the emotions, and in particular the low end of the spectrum. It is important to remember that an emotion has to be provoked from outside, whereas a feeling arises from within.

These people need to be able to accept melancholy, rather than trying to rationalise it or make an enemy of it. They need to enjoy being alone when they are feeling down as much as they enjoy being with others when they are feeling high. The emotional wave in this channel is prone to the pulsing energy of mutation, which can seem very calm until it suddenly 'spikes' up or 'spikes' down. Because of this, these people can appear very calm for long periods, but may also experience sudden unexpected mood swings. This can even be measured in terms of years.

This is a deeply romantic, acoustic channel with a great sensitivity to music. These people need to talk and listen to each other. They love to act out their moods and express their feelings, and because of this they make natural actors, musicians, poets and artists of all kinds.

39 Quarter of Civilisation
THEME: FORM

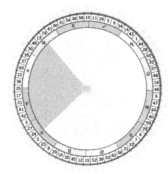

55 Quarter of Initiation
THEME: MIND

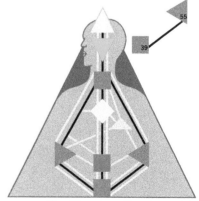

The Knowing Circuit
THE CHANNEL OF EMOTING

THE GATE OF PROVOCATION — OBSTRUCTION

QUICK REFERENCE THEME: People who are here to provoke the spirit of others.

DESCRIPTION: People with this gate are here to provoke the emotions of others in order to see the quality of their spirit. Provocation comes in all kinds of forms; for example, you can even provoke someone by doing nothing (both the 39 and the 55 are Gates of Indecision). Essentially, this is a Gate of Flirting. If these people get a negative reaction to their provocation then the other person's spirit is not in resonance with theirs, and they have to learn not to take that personally.

People with this gate have to learn how to provoke pleasure instead of pain, and joy instead of sadness (although actors with this channel use it to good effect). Their success in eliciting the desired reaction in someone else is directly dependent on the mood of the 39. In other words, if they are in a bad mood they can provoke misery in others, and often without even meaning to.

This is a Gate of Deafness (38,39,43). Like all individuals, these people are reluctant to be influenced by others. However, the 39 needs the 55 in the form of someone to provoke so it can work out what it is feeling. When you provoke someone else's emotions, it also shows you what your own spirit is feeling. 39's are always looking for someone to fall in love with.

As a Root Gate, these people have specific coping strategies for dealing with stress. More often than not, these strategies are rooted in food consumption. In other words, they often try to deal with stress by eating or not eating.

ADVANCED KEYNOTES

Pressure Gate – Pressure to provoke an emotion
Foundation of Hexagram – 39.1 – Disengagement
Personality Sun Crosses – Tension, Provocation, Individualism
Genetic Codon Group – Serine (58,54,53,39,52,15)
Awareness Stream – Stream of Emoting (Fuel of Provocation)

Gate of Sexuality (Emotional) – Gate of needing Sexual Attention, a design of Teasing
Gate of Melancholy – Not knowing whom to provoke
Nutritional – The impulse to eat
Other Keynotes – Gate of Deafness (38,39,43), Indecision (39,55)

THE GATE OF THE SPIRIT — ABUNDANCE

QUICK REFERENCE THEME: People who are deeply melancholic, musical and/or romantic and must honour their moods at all costs.

DESCRIPTION: This gate measures emotional highs and lows, and people who have it defined are always looking for that perfect emotional state, whether it be peace, love or ecstasy. 55's are literally waiting to be provoked (by 39's) in order to know what they are feeling. If their emotional wave is 'up', they feel at home with themselves, if it is 'down' then they feel melancholic. Their cup is always neither half full or half empty.

These people need to let go of trying to rationalise and control their moods. Above all, they must learn not to make up reasons for their emotional chemistry. If they wait out the emotional wave (whether their own or someone else's) they will always have a clearer perception of any situation.

The 55th gate is deeply acoustic and these people are therefore very sensitive to what other people say as well as the tone in which it is said. This is also the Gate of Fickleness, and people who have it defined can appear very sensitive over issues which others do not understand. The 55 can never be wrong in what it feels, but it has to learn not to take anything personally. It is the chemistry of these people that colours everything they hear.

ADVANCED KEYNOTES

Awareness Processing Gate – To know which provocation feels right
Foundation of Hexagram – 55.1 – Cooperation
Personality Sun Crosses – Sleeping Phoenix, Moods, Spirit
Genetic Codon Group – Histidine (49,55)
Awareness Stream – Stream of Emoting (Potential of Spirit)
Gate of Sexuality (Emotional) – Gate of Sexual Moodiness, a design of being Fickle

Gate of Fear – The Fear of feeling Empty
Gate of Nervousness – Nervousness over Moods
Gate of Melancholy – Emptiness leading to potential eating disorders
Gate of Love – The Love of Being in Love
Nutritional – The Mood to eat
Other keynotes – Gate of Indecision (39,55)

THE CHANNEL OF OPENNESS
A DESIGN OF A SOCIAL BEING
CIRCUIT: The Knowing Circuit
CHANNEL TYPE: Manifested Channel

QUICK REFERENCE THEME: Yours is a life of passion and of following your feelings. However, your lesson is to wait before you act or speak. The more patient you are, the clearer your emotions can be and the more powerful your influence.

SEXUALITY KEYNOTE: The Channel of Making Music.

WHOLE CHANNEL: These people are here to have an impact on others through their unique emotional expression. They can be as charming as they can be ferocious.

As this is a Manifesting Channel, these people generally need to inform others before they release their emotions in order to avoid arousing anger and resistance.

They are not so interested in bonding with others as much as finding an opportunity to express themselves – this is a Selfish Individual Channel by design. Their deepest role in life is to have an impact on the emotions of others. However, they can only be really effective at influencing others when they honour their moods absolutely. Their credo is: Don't eat if you're not in the mood; don't go out if you're not in the mood etc…

22 Quarter of Initiation
THEME: MIND

12 Quarter of Civilisation
THEME: FORM

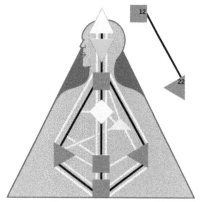

The Knowing Circuit
THE CHANNEL OF OPENNESS

THE GATE OF OPENNESS — GRACE

QUICK REFERENCE THEME: People under huge pressure to express their feelings.

DESCRIPTION: This gate is where the emotional spirit of the individual is transmitted to others as a mood. Although this can be a deeply social gate, these people should stay indoors when in a bad mood! When the emotional wave is high, they are graceful and social, but when the wave is low, their behaviour can be 'dis'graceful or antisocial. Without the 12 this gate is an emotional wave with no way of expressing itself verbally. They may know what they feel, but they may not be able to express it.

These people have the potential to empower others through the depth of their emotion. When their mood is right, they have an almost magnetic natural charm, especially over strangers.

This is the Gate of the Left Ear, which only ever hears according to its wave. This means that these people only ever hear what they feel like hearing. If they want to know something fully, they have to hear it several times over a period of time.

ADVANCED KEYNOTES

Emotional Awareness Gate (potential) – The left ear that only hears what it feels like hearing
Foundation of Hexagram – 22.1 – Second class ticket
Personality Sun Crosses – Rulership, Grace, Informing
Genetic Codon Group – Proline (37,63,22,36)
Awareness Stream – Stream of Emoting (Possibility of Social Spirit)
Gate of Sexuality (Emotional) – Gate of Attentiveness, a design of Infatuation
Gate of Fear – The Fear of Silence and lack of Growth

Gate of Nervousness – Nervousness over Openness
Gate of Melancholy – Melancholy that there is nothing worth listening to
Nutritional – Digestive Prana
Design of Forms – Human emotional connection to mammals – Food seduction – The Breeders (provoking openness)
Other keynotes – Gate of Strangers, Disgrace, Laughing & Crying

 # THE GATE OF CAUTION — STANDSTILL

QUICK REFERENCE THEME: People who are naturally cautious about other people understanding them clearly.

DESCRIPTION: Those with this gate can be extremely articulate when their mood is right. If they are able to express themselves clearly, then their words and actions can have a profound emotional impact on others. Here the mutation potential comes through the tone and vibration of the voice, rather than the words themselves. This gate needs the 22 because this is a voice seeking to express a deep emotional truth. Without the 22, these are people who know how to express themselves but don't necessarily know what it is they are feeling. They have to wait to be clear about their feelings.

Because this is an acoustic channel, when these people begin to talk, they can actually hear the emotional quality through their tone (whether the wave is theirs or someone else's), but until they talk, they cannot know.

This is also the Gate of Silence. These people can use the auric power of their silence to influence others.

ADVANCED KEYNOTES

Expression Gate – Manifestation of openness or not
Voice – I Act/Try (mood dependent)
Foundation of Hexagram – 12.1 – The Monk
Personality Sun Crosses – Eden, Articulation, Education
Genetic Codon Group – Stop Codon Group (12,33,56)
Awareness Stream – Stream of Emoting (Expression of Caution)
Gate of Sexuality (Emotional) – Gate of Romanticism, a design of Caution/Abandon

Gate of Melancholy – Melancholy that there is no one worth telling anything to
Gate of Aloneness – (40,33,12)
Dreamrave Key – Portal Bridge – Mutation
Nutritional – Eating Prana Regulator
Design of Forms – Cross Species Gate – Readiness to eat or be eaten (mammals)
Other keynotes – Silence, Stuttering, Breath

THE CHANNEL OF MUTATION
A DESIGN OF ENERGY WHICH INITIATES AND FLUCTUATES – PULSE

CIRCUIT: The Knowing Circuit
CHANNEL TYPE: Generated Channel

QUICK REFERENCE THEME: Wherever you are physically present, there is always a chance of something new coming into the world. The price you pay for this gift is to accept the limitation of not knowing when the next quantum leap will come.

WHOLE CHANNEL: The agents of evolution itself, these people are here to bring radical change into the world. They bring something new to everything they touch, and are always under pressure to change the way things are done.

These are people who can be totally unpredictable and can at any point suddenly change their whole direction. They force everyone around them to grow and adapt to the changes that they bring. These are auras that engender either innovation and/or instability in others. As long as they are responding to life and not jumping according to the wishes of their minds, they can always trust the impact they have on their environment.

People who have this definition in their design are moving from order to chaos and back again endlessly. The fixed on/off pulse energy of this channel will dominate the rest of their design, colouring the frequency of all other channels with its innovation and instability.

Because of their unpredictable chemistry, these people can be deeply melancholic but very creative. They sporadically go into dark spaces within themselves, often where they feel they cannot see or understand anything. At such times they can feel frustrated or stuck, as though everything in their life has stopped dead. These kinds of feelings are natural for these people, and they have to love the dark periods as much as the light, because every time they emerge from the darkness they will emerge as a totally fresh person.

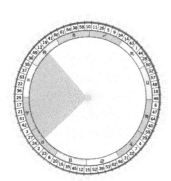

3 Quarter of Initiation
THEME: MIND

60 Quarter of Mutation
THEME: TRANSFORMATION

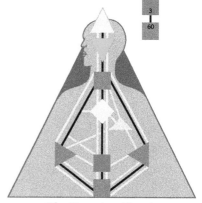

The Knowing Circuit
THE CHANNEL OF MUTATION

THE GATE OF ORDERING — DIFFICULTY AT THE BEGINING

QUICK REFERENCE THEME: People who have to respect that bringing order out of chaos is a process which takes time.

DESCRIPTION: These people are always ready to do something new. They are like a river without banks or structure. There is potential chaos if they do not wait for the right moment and conditions for their potential to emerge. They must weather the frustration of waiting for the 60th gate, which controls the timing of when and how things can be actualised in the outer world.

The 3 needs the discipline and limitation of the 60 to channel its energy into something of lasting value. These are people who need Structure in their lives. If these people are not able to accept the natural limitations of Structure, then their innovative quality will never have a lasting impact in the world.

The melancholy of the 3rd gate is about feeling held back by the rigidity of the physical realm, whether that be someone who will not change their ways to accommodate change, or an old system that holds back a new possibility.

ADVANCED KEYNOTES

Pressure Release Gate – The power to mutate something new
Format Energy Gate – On/Off Pulse
Foundation of Hexagram – 3.1 – Synthesis
Personality Sun Crosses – Laws, Mutation, Wishes
Genetic Codon Group – Leucine (42,3,27,24,20,23)
Gate of Melancholy – Melancholy about nothing ever lasting

Design of Forms – Cellular Mutation on/off switch (single cell)
Gate of potential Depression – Why am I deeply confused?
Mystical Gate (WA) – Gate of the New
Food Type – Sugars (rushes and hits)
Other keynotes – Gate of Biological and Cultural Mutation

THE GATE OF ACCEPTANCE — LIMITATION

QUICK REFERENCE THEME: People with the potential to bring lasting changes into the world.

DESCRIPTION: This is the pulsing pressure to mutate, i.e. to bring something totally new into the world. This energy pulses on and off sporadically, and the mutation happens in the gaps between.

These people feel a great pressure within them to innovate something new, but cannot release it whenever they please; hence it is the Gate of Accepting Limitation. The great challenge of this gate is to learn to wait for the right moment without knowing when it will come or even what it will bring. While these people are waiting for the next gearshift in life, they can become deeply melancholic. Ironically, it is at such times, when they feel at their most limited, that the mutation within them is occurring; like the butterfly hidden within the chrysalis.

Without the presence of the 3rd gate, these people can feel very held back by life. If they are able to accept these feelings, they can transform them into creative endeavours and structures that will ultimately be of huge benefit when the next mutation in their life finally arrives.

ADVANCED KEYNOTES

Pressure Gate – Pulse energy, pressure to mutate
Format Energy Gate – On/Off Pulse
Foundation of Hexagram – 60.1 – Acceptance
Personality Sun Crosses – Laws, Limitation, Distraction
Genetic Codon Group – Isoleucine (60,61,19)
Gate of Melancholy – Melancholy about having nowhere to go

Mystical Gate (WA) – Gate of the Old
Gate of potential Depression – Why am I stuck in limitation?
Food Type – Sugars (rushes and hits)
Other keynotes – Gate of Restraint, Structure, Innovation

THE CHANNEL OF THE BEAT
A DESIGN OF BEING A KEEPER OF THE KEYS
CIRCUIT: The Knowing Circuit
CHANNEL TYPE: Generated Channel

QUICK REFERENCE THEME: Because you have the ability and power to always follow your own direction in life, you are a 'wayshower' for others, whether directly or indirectly.

WHOLE CHANNEL: People who have this channel defined have both the energy to sustain creative work and the gift of knowing how to use their work to empower others. These are people who have an in-built mission in life. As long as they are waiting to respond to life as they go along, their direction will always unfold naturally. Whereas the channel 3/60 is simply a blind pressure to create change, people with this 2/14 channel have the skill to manipulate change in the direction they wish.

These people have very powerful auric fields that can directly affect the direction of other people's lives. At times, this can be very subtle – for example, you can pass through the aura of a 2/14 and undergo a change in your own direction.

This is one of the three Tantric Channels. In this instance, tantra refers to the need to surrender to the inner direction of the Sacral Centre. This can be experienced as life itself making decisions, rather than a conscious participation in decision-making. It can be a profound experience for such people when they let go and trust life.

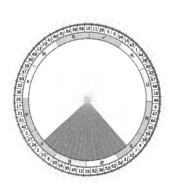

2 Quarter of Civilisation
THEME: FORM

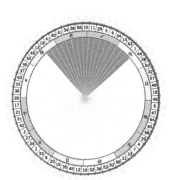

14 Quarter of Mutation
THEME: TRANSFORMATION

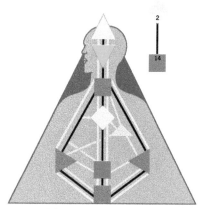

The Knowing Circuit
THE CHANNEL OF THE BEAT

THE GATE OF DIRECTION OF THE SELF – THE RECEPTIVE

QUICK REFERENCE THEME: People with a flair for innovative guidance.

DESCRIPTION: These people have an inherent alignment for where someone or something needs to go. The power of this gate can be symbolised by the acorn that knows how to become an oak tree, but needs the sunlight and water of the 14 (resources and commitment) to make it happen.

These people know where they want to go, but lack the ability to get there without the 14. This is the key that starts the engine of the 14. These are people that can get frustrated or exhausted from trying to do all the work themselves. They are not the ones who are necessarily here to do the work. Rather, they hold the gift of coordinating where and how the creative process can be directed. The secret for such people is to find the right allies in life in order that they can use their gifts.

ADVANCED KEYNOTES

Role Gate – The director, the driver
Foundation of Hexagram – 2.1 – Intuition
Personality Sun Crosses – Sphinx, Driver, Defiance
Genetic Codon Group – Phenylalanine (2,8)
Gate of the Sphinx – The Seat of the Magnetic Monopole

Gate of Melancholy – Melancholy about things not moving fast enough
Mystical Gate (WA) – The Planner
Other keynotes – The Higher Self, Director, Driver

THE GATE OF POWER SKILLS – POSSESSION IN GREAT MEASURE

QUICK REFERENCE THEME: People whose creative potential lies in loving the work that they do.

DESCRIPTION: This gate represents the power to find your unique direction in life. These people have the skills and commitment to drive new projects and creative endeavours out into the world. People with this gate are here to work in life, but they have to find work that for them is a labour of love. This is also a Gate of Wealth because it has the power to generate wealth through sustained creative work.

The 14 always needs the 2 in order to give it a viable direction. The 14 alone is the pure potential to keep working, but without the presence of the 2 these people can get caught into working endlessly with no real sense of where they are going. This is also the Gate of Slavery.

ADVANCED KEYNOTES

Energy Control Gate – The 'turbine'
Foundation of Hexagram – 14.1 – Money isn't everything
Personality Sun Crosses – Contagion, Empowering, Uncertainty
Genetic Codon Group – Lysine (14,1)

Gate of Melancholy – Melancholy about having to work or not
Mystical Gate (WA) – The Empowerer
Other keynotes – Gate of Wealth (The Wagon), Slavery, Workaholics

THE CHANNEL OF INSPIRATION
A DESIGN OF BEING A CREATIVE ROLE MODEL
CIRCUIT: The Knowing Circuit (Creative Channel)
CHANNEL TYPE: Projected Channel

QUICK REFERENCE THEME: You are here to be creatively different from everyone else. Your life is about having the courage to stand out from the crowd. Simply by being yourself, you will always get the recognition you deserve.

WHOLE CHANNEL: These people have natural creative abilities and the skill to express them in a unique way. They are individuals who empower others by being different and inspirational.

This is the Creative Channel of the Knowing Circuit. These people can bring such unusual creativity into the world that they can end up becoming role models who inspire others to be equally bold. Like the 13/33 and the 7/31, this is also a Channel of Leadership, although these people are not particularly interested in being followed. They simply set an example of someone who knows where they are going.

These people can impact the public with a wonderful sense of creative and unusual presence, for example, they may look or dress differently from the crowd. There is nothing worse for a 1/8 person to be told by someone else that they remind them of someone. They are here to be unique! Since this is a Projected Channel, they need to be recognised and invited to express their uniqueness in order to earn the respect that they deserve.

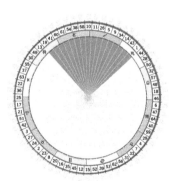

1 Quarter of Mutation
THEME: TRANSFORMATION

8 Quarter of Civilisation
THEME: FORM

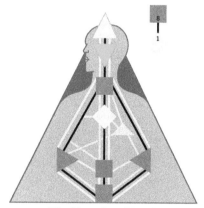

The Knowing Circuit
THE CHANNEL OF INSPIRATION

THE GATE OF SELF EXPRESSION – THE CREATIVE

QUICK REFERENCE THEME: People who have an immense capacity for creativity.

DESCRIPTION: This is the Gate of the Creative Artist – these people have a design that always attracts attention, yet paradoxically have a need to work alone. Their creativity is always rooted in a philosophy of "I have to do it my way". Such creativity waxes and wanes and can emerge or disappear in the blink of an eye.

These people are here to create for the sake of creativity, rather than for any recognition that may come their way. Ironically, when they simply become immersed in their creativity without a thought for any goal, they have the best chance of actually being discovered. Metaphorically, the 8 represents their agent.

Whilst the 1 is the artist, the 8 knows how to market the art.

ADVANCED KEYNOTES

Role Gate – Projection of unique creative self-expression
Foundation of Hexagram – 1.1 – Creation is Independent of Will
Personality Sun Crosses – Sphinx, Self-Expression, Defiance
Genetic Codon Group – Lysine (1,14)
Gate of the Sphinx – Direction in the Now

Gate of Melancholy – Melancholy about not being seen as being different
Dreamrave Key – Joy (Light Field)
Design of Forms – Mutation through unique individual direction/expression (Mammals, Birds, Reptiles and Fish)
Other keynotes – The Artist/Creator

THE GATE OF CONTRIBUTION – HOLDING TOGETHER

QUICK REFERENCE THEME: People with a gift of knowing how to draw people's attention to a truth.

DESCRIPTION: The agent – these people always have a need to express their own individual contribution, as well as that of others. They are looking for someone or something to promote. They have the ability to stand up and get everyone's attention. Even if no one follows them, they will continue on their own unique path alone.

Without the 1st gate these people are always looking for the inspirational qualities of the creator/leader. However, their role is not so much to bear the burden of leadership as be the promoter of something or someone new.

ADVANCED KEYNOTES

Expression Gate – Unique Self Expression
Voice – "I know I can make a contribution"
Foundation of Hexagram – 8.1 – Honesty
Personality Sun Crosses – Contagion, Contribution, Uncertainty
Genetic Codon Group – Phenylalanine (8,2)
Gate of Melancholy – Melancholy about no one paying them attention

Dreamrave Key – Darkness (Light Field)
Design of Forms – Manifestation of Individuality – The Call of the Wild (Mammals) – Imprinting (Birds, Reptiles, Fish)
Other keynotes – The Agent

THE CHANNEL OF EXPLORATION
A DESIGN OF FOLLOWING ONE'S CONVICTIONS
CIRCUIT: Centering Circuit (Creative Channel)
CHANNEL TYPE: Generated Channel

QUICK REFERENCE THEME: Your purpose in life is to love yourself and life enough to trust in your inner convictions, no matter how senseless they may seem to others.

WHOLE CHANNEL: These people are here to do only what they love in life, and when they can trust in this they truly display their power. Since this is the Creative Channel of the Centering Circuit, these people are deeply creative when following their own convictions. As long as they do not impose their own way on others, these are truly empowering individuals. Their rare ability to invoke the inner strength within others derives from their own belief and love of themselves.

People with this channel can uplift the people around them by bringing them more deeply into themselves. In other words, they make people more independent and less reliant on others. This is what it means to be centred. These people can at the same time be very selfish, always wanting to go their own way regardless of what others think or say. If they are living their design, they have no need to feel guilty about this.

These people do not need to be aware of why they behave in their own unique way. Neither do they have to question their own behaviour, even though others probably do. By surrendering to their own inner responses to life, moment by moment, they will always be in the right place and at the right time.

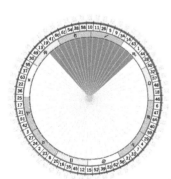

34 Quarter of Mutation
THEME: TRANSFORMATION

10 Quarter of Mutation
THEME: TRANSFORMATION

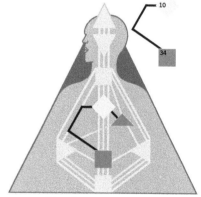

The Centering Circuit
THE CHANNEL OF EXPLORATION

34 THE GATE OF POWER — THE POWER OF THE GREAT

QUICK REFERENCE THEME: People whose actions are generally independent and self-centred, but who do not need to feel guilty about the fact.

DESCRIPTION: This is a gate of pure vital energy that emerges naturally out of response to external stimuli. It is a Gate of Self-empowerment; through the intuition (when connected to the 57), through behaviour (when connected to the 10) and through activity (when connected to the 20).

This gate is rooted in the urge to display how different one is from others. It fuels the survival of the individual and is the only Asexual Gate coming from the sacral. Unlike all the other gates of the sacral, this is the only gate of being unavailable. This manifests as someone being unavailable because they are busy (when connected to the 34), unavailable because they are following their own convictions (when connected to the 10) or unavailable to listen (when connected to the 57).

Without the 57, the 34 is always a power that is unaware of itself and therefore can potentially be dangerous to itself or others.

ADVANCED KEYNOTES

Energy Display Gate – Self-empowerment, independence
Foundation of Hexagram – 34.1 – The Bully
Genetic Codon Group – Asparagine (34,43)
Gate of Sexuality (Caring) – Gate of Individuation (unavailable for caring)

Gate of Melancholy – Frustration at not being able to use one's power in the Now
Design of Forms – The power to proliferate (birds, reptiles, fish)
Other Keynotes – Unavailable through being Self-absorbed

10 THE GATE OF BEHAVIOUR OF THE SELF — TREADING

QUICK REFERENCE THEME: People whose lives are an expression of their own uniqueness – The Love of Oneself.

DESCRIPTION: One of the Gates of Love, this gate is about the love of being oneself. When the 10 is connected to the 34 it emerges as individualised creative living.

These people are here to express one of six behaviour patterns, according to which 10th gate line they have: the Investigator (1), the Hermit (2), the Martyr (3), the Opportunist (4), the Heretic (5) and the Role Model (6).

When the gate is not part of a defined channel, these people are often deeply concerned about the behaviour of others.

ADVANCED KEYNOTES

Primary Role Gate – The 6 behavioural roles
Gate of the Vessel of Love – The love of being oneself – The lip of the vessel, through which life pours
Foundation of Hexagram – 10.1 – Modesty
Personality Sun Crosses – Vessel of Love, Behaviour, Prevention
Genetic Codon Group – Arginine (25,17,21,51,38,10)

Gate of Melancholy – Melancholy that no one else knows how to behave
Mystical Gate – 'The Li' – The love of the Way
Gate of Sexuality (Caring) – Self Love or not
Design of Forms – Love as Form and Beauty (plants)
Other Keynotes – The Chameleon, The Winter Solstice

THE CHANNEL OF INITIATION
A DESIGN OF NEEDING TO BE FIRST
CIRCUIT: Centering Circuit (Creative Channel)
CHANNEL TYPE: Projected Channel

QUICK REFERENCE THEME: Your life is a series of leaps into the unknown. You are born with the spirit of a warrior, and you are here to learn to walk your path on your own. Take courage, leap when the need calls and worry about the consequences afterwards!

MYSTICAL KEYNOTE CHANNEL: The Channel of Mystical Direction, a design of Leaping into The Void.

WHOLE CHANNEL: In the mundane world, these people are deeply competitive. By going into new arenas, stretching themselves beyond their normal limits, shocking themselves and others, they are here to feel the wonder of their own unique spirit.

These people also like to test the limits of their endurance and can end up transcending their own sense of power into a totally fresh (even mystical) experience of themselves. (The 34/10 doesn't transcend, it only feels its power through displaying it before others).

These are people who can initiate others into doing things that they wouldn't normally do. They love to be the first to enter a new arena and they carry a powerful design in the business world, where they empower organisations through their individual flair and 'gutsy' approach to getting what they want.

25 Quarter of Initiation
THEME: MIND

51 Quarter of Initiation
THEME: MIND

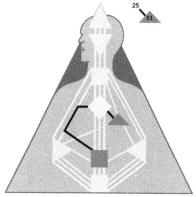

The Centering Circuit
THE CHANNEL OF INITIATION

THE GATE OF THE SPIRIT OF THE SELF – INNOCENCE

QUICK REFERENCE THEME: People for whom true initiation is to retain innocence despite circumstances.

DESCRIPTION: This is the Gate of Universal, Unconditional Love. This kind of love is a 'cool' love, as opposed to the hot love of the 46. People with this gate defined are capable of a deep compassion for all life, although not necessarily for any one individual over another. Such people are always looking for the excitement and thrill of the 51. If they wait, they will get their fair share of excitement.

These are people who are consistently initiated by life. They undergo many challenges that test and deepen their innocence. The result of facing such challenges is a deeper kind of innocence, like that of an old man compared to a child.

ADVANCED KEYNOTES

Gate of the Vessel of Love – Universal Love – The Blood within the Vessel
Foundation of Hexagram – 25.1 – Selflessness
Personality Sun Crosses – Vessel of Love, Innocence, Healing
Genetic Codon Group – Arginine (10,38,25,17,21,51)
Mystical Gate – The Consecration and the Blood

Mystical Gate (WA) – The Shaman, The Priestess
Gate Of Melancholy – Melancholy about being Insignificant
Design of Forms – The Law of Existence – The Blood of the Universe (Inanimate)
Nutritional – The Blood (Liver)
Other Keynotes – Spring Equinox

 # THE GATE OF SHOCK – THE AROUSING

QUICK REFERENCE THEME: People who need to test themselves in order to be either best or first at something.

DESCRIPTION: This is the Gate of Individual Initiative – it is the only gate out of the Heart/Ego Centre that is not part of the Tribal Circuitry.

These are people with very competitive energy which can manifest as either foolhardiness or courage. They love to shock people with their love of going where no one else dares. They are always looking for the 25, a sense of spirit or the feeling of going beyond themselves. These people bring a sense of unpredictability and excitement to life, and they have a particular gift of empowering others by shocking them out of their own little worlds and into the bigger picture.

ADVANCED KEYNOTES

Ego Potential Gate – The will to compete
Foundation of Hexagram – 51.1 – Reference
Personality Sun Crosses – Penetration, Shock, Clarion
Genetic Codon Group – Arginine (10,38,25,17,21,51)
Mystical Gate – The Warrior's Heart and the readiness for battle

Mystical Gate (WA) – The Spiritual Warrior/Fool
Gate Of Melancholy – Melancholy about lack of excitement
Nutritional – The Gall (Gall Bladder)
Other Keynotes – Gate of Thunder (Chinese), Courage

THE CHANNEL OF LOGIC
A DESIGN OF MENTAL EASE MIXED WITH DOUBT
CIRCUIT: The Understanding Circuit
CHANNEL TYPE: Projected Channel

QUICK REFERENCE THEME: You are always healthiest using your mental gifts in the service of others, rather than trying to understand your own life. If you wait, there will always be someone who needs your clarity and inspiration.

WHOLE CHANNEL: This channel represents the scientific, sceptical mind that has to question the logical validity of everything. These people are under constant mental pressure to come up with logical answers to their doubts.

Ultimately these people are here to bring inspiration by questioning and filtering mental patterns, and by looking for inconsistencies in order to protect us from misjudgement in the future. The answers they come up with are not necessarily the right ones, and ideally they must be tested and proved before they have any practical value.

These kinds of minds are always focussed on the future, and thus these people can worry a great deal about their own future. The only way to avoid this anxiety is to use their minds for research purposes keeping them busy thinking about other things.

These are people who ideally need to wait to be invited before they express their doubts and/or solutions, otherwise they may end up giving others a headache!

63 Quarter of Initiation
THEME: MIND

4 Quarter of Duality
THEME: RELATIONSHIPS

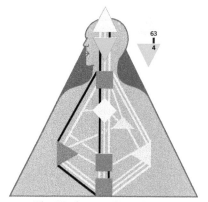

The Understanding Circuit
THE CHANNEL OF LOGIC

THE GATE OF DOUBT – AFTER COMPLETION

QUICK REFERENCE THEME: People born with naturally sceptical minds.

DESCRIPTION: This is the Gate of Questioning, as well as the pressure of needing an answer. These people can be suspicious and distrustful until they have questioned the logic of something for themselves.

It is the insatiable pressure of the doubt in this gate that drives all scientific thought. Such people can be the source of much that is useful to the world. However, if this doubt is turned inwards on oneself, it is deeply disturbing.

These people need to wait for the 4 in order to find a resolution to the doubt, since the 4 comes up with the answer, which temporarily relieves the pressure on the 63. If you are a 63 with no 4, you carry questions that you have no need of answering yourself. Your questions are here to inspire others rather than confuse you.

ADVANCED KEYNOTES

Pressure Gate – The pressure to doubt and question
Foundation of Hexagram – 63.1 – Composure
Personality Sun Crosses – Consciousness, Doubts, Dominion
Genetic Codon Group – Proline (37,63,22,36)

Awareness Stream – Stream of Understanding (Fuel of Doubt)
Other Keynotes – Gate of Madness and Dreaming (61,63,64)

 # THE GATE OF FORMULISATION – YOUTHFUL FOLLY

QUICK REFERENCE THEME: People who will always need questions to resolve.

DESCRIPTION: People with this gate like to come up with answers to the questions raised by the 63. At this stage in the circuitry, the answers are still only concepts and have yet to be tested out and verified. Because of this, many of the answers that such people come out with are sheer folly, and are not necessarily solutions or facts, but simply a release of the mental pressure they feel.

These are people who often experience anxiety when their minds do not understand something. Once they do understand something, it is always replaced with another question, and so the process goes on. As with the 63, the questions and potential answers that are part of this channel are not meant for the individual, but are to be shared with others.

People with the 4 but no 63 are people with a potential answer for every problem except their own.

ADVANCED KEYNOTES

Conceptual Processing Gate – The struggle to come up with an answer
Foundation of Hexagram – 4.1 – Pleasure
Personality Sun Crosses – Explanation, Formulisation, Revolution
Genetic Codon Group – Valine (59,29,4,7)

Awareness Stream – Stream of Understanding (Potential to formulise)
Gate of Fear – The Fear of Chaos
Gate of Anxiety – Anxiety over Doubts
Other Keynotes – The Gate of Answers, Doubting Thomas, Suspiciousness

THE CHANNEL OF ACCEPTANCE
A DESIGN OF AN ORGANISATIONAL BEING
CIRCUIT: The Understanding Circuit
CHANNEL TYPE: Projected Channel

QUICK REFERENCE THEME: You have the rare mental ability of seeing the bigger picture without getting bogged down in the details. However, if you do not take the time to look into all the relevant facts and details, your long term visions will inevitably falter.

WHOLE CHANNEL: These people need all the facts at their fingertips before they speak. Their opinions have to be backed up by detail. If they wait to be invited to speak, they can fascinate others with their detail and knowledge. If not, they can equally bore people with all kinds of unnecessary detail.

Many 17/62s have a weak right eye because they have been trying to share their opinions for most of their lives without waiting to be invited, thus they slowly destroy their capacity to see patterns clearly.

These are natural organisers of others, who are here to develop and improve logical patterns for the future. They are logical think tanks with managerial skills, though only at a mental level. Since these are visually oriented people, they work best with images. Their eye has the ability to see all the working parts of any structure, detect potential flaws and profer their opinion as to a possible solution based on detailed knowledge of the subject. These collective gifts are very sought after by many organisations.

17 Quarter of Initiation
THEME: MIND

62 Quarter of Civilisation
THEME: FORM

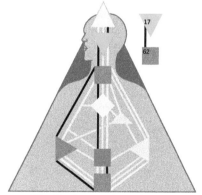

The Understanding Circuit
THE CHANNEL OF ACCEPTANCE

THE GATE OF OPINION – FOLLOWING

QUICK REFERENCE THEME: People who form opinions by projecting their minds into the future, in order to be of service.

DESCRIPTION: Having logical minds, these people need to organise the solution to their doubts into a workable concept ready to be expressed to others. They have to shape a new opinion out of a mental pattern so that it can withstand both testing and criticism. This is the Gate of the Right Eye and pattern recognition. The 17 takes the answer to the doubt from the 63/4 and forms an opinion from it. However, opinions at this stage of the conceptual process are merely theoretical and require the presence of the 62 to provide the detail and hard fact in order to back them up.

These kinds of people have an eye for seeing and understanding structures and frameworks, but no instant ability to share what they have understood. The way the eye sees something is often very difficult to translate without an image. These are visually oriented people. This is also the Gate of Time Distortion – these people often have an unusual sense of timing.

ADVANCED KEYNOTES

Conceptual Crystallisation Gate – Visualisation of what mental pattern is correct or not (the right eye)
Foundation of Hexagram – 17.1 – Openness
Personality Sun Crosses – Service, Opinions, Upheaval
Genetic Codon Group – Arginine (10,38,25,17,21,51)
Awareness Stream – Stream of Understanding (Possibility of Opinions)

Gate of Fear – The Fear of being Challenged
Gate of Anxiety – Anxiety over Detail
Design Of Forms – Human mental/vocal connection to mammals – The Tamers – Conditioning Patterns
Other Keynotes – Gate of Time Distortion

 # THE GATE OF DETAILS –
THE PREPONDERANCE OF THE SMALL

QUICK REFERENCE THEME: People with an eye for detail and who always need to know the facts.

DESCRIPTION: This is the gate that assembles, organises and labels the details of things in life in order that formulae can be clearly expressed. These people have an eye for picking out very precise (and sometimes obscure) details in complex situations.

The gift of these people is to explain the intangible, making it accessible through clear factual expression. This is also the Gate of Naming. Without the 17, these people may have all the details of a situation but no ability to put them into a stuctural context.

This is also a Cross-species Gate – these are people with the potential to communicate with and train animals.

ADVANCED KEYNOTES

Conceptual Expression Gate – Verbal expression of mental pattern
Voice – I Think
Foundation of Hexagram – 62.1 – Routine
Personality Sun Crosses – Maya, Detail, Obscuration
Genetic Codon Group – Tyrosine (32,62)

Awareness Stream – Stream of Understanding (Expression of Fact)
Design Of Forms – Cross Species Gate – Adaption/ Communication (Mammals)
Dreamrave Key – Portal/Bridge – Love (Light Field)
Other Keynotes – Gate of Naming, Facts

48/16 THE CHANNEL OF THE WAVELENGTH
A DESIGN OF TALENT
CIRCUIT: The Understanding Circuit (Creative Channel)
CHANNEL TYPE: Projected Channel

QUICK REFERENCE THEME: You have the design of Talent, but this talent has to be earned through constant repetition and gradual improvement. Wait to find the one thing you can give yourself to totally.

SEXUALITY KEYNOTE: The Channel of Caring Skills.

WHOLE CHANNEL: Being the Creative Channel of the Understanding Circuit, the 48/16 is about mastery – these people are here to find something in life that they can practice over and over until they have refined and mastered it.

Logical creativity is different from individual creativity. This channel represents talent that has to be earned by hard work and commitment. If these people are able to stay with their process, their recognition will always finally come. Thus, mastery always depends on continual repetition, but it eventually becomes art when it is liberated from technique. It takes the body 7 years to learn any technique deeply enough in order to transcend it.

As a channel of the Understanding Circuit, the talent in this channel is here to be shared with the collective. Such talent is most natural when it has a wider purpose that improves the world in some way. This is also the Channel of Caring Skills.

48 Quarter of Duality
THEME: RELATIONSHIPS

16 Quarter of Civilisation
THEME: FORM

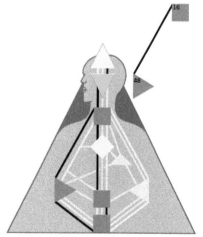

The Understanding Circuit
THE CHANNEL OF WAVELENGTH

48 THE GATE OF DEPTH — THE WELL

QUICK REFERENCE THEME: People born with a wisdom so natural that they rarely see it themselves until someone asks.

DESCRIPTION: These people always have the potential to come up with new solutions for things. Whereas the 58 is the blind joy of challenging something and the 18 is the ability to pinpoint that challenge specifically through criticism, it takes the 48 to suggest an actual solution to any problem. People with a 48 in their design are sitting on a fount of natural wisdom waiting for the right moment to be shared.

Without the presence of the 16th gate 48's have no clear way of recognising their depth, and thus no ability or skills to apply it to the world. This is why this is the Gate of Inadequacy. The fear of this gate is twofold; that their wisdom may never emerge when it is called upon – and that they may not possess the skills to express this depth in the first place.

As with all Projected Channels, if these people wait for others to initiate and recognise their depth, it will emerge clearly and correctly.

ADVANCED KEYNOTES

Awareness Crystalisation Gate – The depth to correct the pattern
Foundation of Hexagram – 48.1 – Insignificance
Personality Sun Crosses – Tension, Depth, Endeavour
Genetic Codon Group – Alanine (57,48,18,46)

Awareness Stream – Stream of Taste (Possibility of a solution)
Gate of Sexuality (Caring) – Gate of Caring Frustration, a design of a lack of Experimentation
Gate of Fear – The Fear of Inadequacy
Other Keynotes – Gate of Black Magick, Solutions

16 THE GATE OF SKILLS — ENTHUSIASM

QUICK REFERENCE THEME: People who can never have enough skills. They are skilled in having many skills.

DESCRIPTION: This gate represents the honing of artistic or scientific skill through repetition. These people have the enthusiasm to experiment with a repetitive process that can lead to mastery. In order to attain mastery of any skill, these people have to be fully identified with that skill. This is the dancer who can become the dance, transcending their skill.

This is the gate where both logical formulae from the mental field and intuitive solutions from the spleen are tested and verified. Without the 48 these people may not know what to experiment on. They may have many skills but are always looking for depth and knowledge from the 48, which provides the foundation to which the skills can be applied.

ADVANCED KEYNOTES

Expression Gate – The development of skill through experimentation and expression
Voice – I Experiment
Foundation of Hexagram – 16.1 – Delusion
Personality Sun Crosses – Planning, Experimentation, Identification

Genetic Codon Group – Cysteine (16,45)
Awareness Stream – Stream of Taste (Expression of Skill)
Gate of Sexuality (Caring) – Gate of Caring Discrimination, a design of Identification
Other Keynotes – Gate of the Arts, Music, Dance

THE CHANNEL OF JUDGEMENT
A DESIGN OF INSATIABILITY
CIRCUIT: The Understanding Circuit
CHANNEL TYPE: Projected Channel

QUICK REFERENCE THEME: As someone who loves to challenge everything in life, you are recommended not to offer your criticism unless asked. Once asked, you will never encounter resistance from others.

SEXUALITY KEYNOTE: The Channel of Correction.

WHOLE CHANNEL: These people are perfectionists. These are logical people who are here to 'bring judgement' in order to improve things for the sake of the whole. They are insatiable in their energy to improve. The trick for them is to realise that their drive to find perfection is designed to only be of service in the public sector, rather than in their personal life. When they have no one or nothing to challenge, their sense of dissatisfaction can turn itself inwards, either on themselves or their friends and families. These people can end up with all kinds of relationship and family problems if they are constantly challenging their closest allies.

As with all the channels between the Root Centre and the Spleen, these people have a regular need for physical exercise in order to burn energy.

Without the 48th gate (the Gate of Depth), these people can show where things have gone wrong and are ready to work on potential improvements, but they do not necessarily know what to replace an established pattern with. In other words, their role is not to come up with a solution, but only to show where the fault lies.

They have to learn that it is the perfecting process that is important rather than the results. For true perfectionists perfection can never actually exist. There are only ascending levels of mastery.

18 Quarter of Duality
THEME: RELATIONSHIPS

58 Quarter of Mutation
THEME: TRANSFORMATION

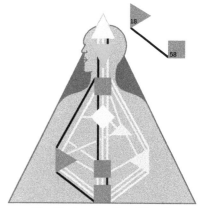

The Understanding Circuit
THE CHANNEL OF JUDGEMENT

THE GATE OF CORRECTION – WORK ON WHAT HAS BEEN SPOILT

QUICK REFERENCE THEME: People with a gift for always seeing the faults in everything in order to make improvements.

DESCRIPTION: These people always see what is wrong with things. They naturally know when any pattern is flawed and feel happiest when challenging it. These are gifted critics. However, without the 58 their tendency is only to see the faults in things without having the drive to do anything about them.

It is through this gate that we receive our deepest conditioning from our parents (regardless of whether we have it defined or not). The greatest conditioning will always come from the parent of the opposite sex.

People with definition in this gate or channel have to confront their parental conditioning over the course of their lives. They need to learn that the very conditioning they received as children is actually the source of their gift of criticism.

This gate represents the fear of authority and the challenge to that authority.

ADVANCED KEYNOTES

Awareness Processing Gate – What is worth challenging or not
Foundation of Hexagram – 18.1 – Conservatism
Personality Sun Crosses – Service, Correction, Upheaval
Genetic Codon Group – Alanine (57,48,18,46)
Awareness Stream – Stream of Taste

(Potential for correction)
Gate of Fear – The Fear of Authority
Gate of Sexuality (Caring) – Gate of Instructive Caring, a design of Challenging
Other Keynotes – Gate of Bitching, Gossip, Perfectionists

 # THE GATE OF VITALITY – THE JOYOUS

QUICK REFERENCE THEME: People with a love of challenging authority simply for the joy of the challenge.

DESCRIPTION: These people have a zest for life which manifests as the drive to improve things in the world around them. This gate represents the vitality to challenge conditioning and is rooted in not being satisfied in the Now. This is the Channel of Insatiability, and this gate is the source of that energy.

Without the 18, these are people whose love of life makes them desperate to be of service in some wider way. They feel the pressure of needing to commit their energy to a process, but on their own they do not possess the clear awareness of how improvements can be made. If they follow their strategy, they will naturally draw the 18's into their lives.

ADVANCED KEYNOTES

Pressure Gate – The pressure to be of service
Foundation of Hexagram – 58.1 – The Love of Life
Personality Sun Crosses – Service, Vitality, Demands
Genetic Codon Group – Serine (58,54,53,39,52,15)
Awareness Stream – Stream of Taste (Fuel of Vitality)

Gate of Sexuality (Caring) – Gate of Caring Vitality, a design of Speculating
Gate of Love – The Love of Perfection
Other Keynotes – Fuel for Repetition

THE CHANNEL OF CONCENTRATION
A DESIGN OF DETERMINATION

CIRCUIT: The Understanding Circuit
CHANNEL TYPE: Generated Channel

QUICK REFERENCE THEME: The ideal of your life is to use your powers of concentration in the service of improving something that will make a difference in the world.

WHOLE CHANNEL: These people are here to bring a determination and focus to anything they do. They are here to hold together any endeavour and concentrate their entire being into any process. They bring focus to any group that they are a part of.

As one of the 3 format energies in the body, this is a very powerful energy and wherever it is present in someone's design, it greatly intensifies all other channels in the bodygraph.

These people hate having to put their energy into several things at the same time. They need to respond to the pressure that makes them quiet and still. Then they can enter a space where they can concentrate all their energy into a detailed process.

The potential for depression here is: "Why can't I move?"(the 52 without the 9) or "Why can't I sit still and focus?" (the 9 without the 52).

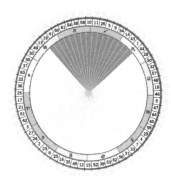

9 Quarter of Mutation
THEME: TRANSFORMATION

52 Quarter of Civilisation
THEME: FORM

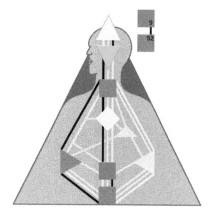

The Understanding Circuit
THE CHANNEL OF CONCENTRATION

THE GATE OF FOCUS –
THE TAMING POWER OF THE SMALL

QUICK REFERENCE THEME: People with an ability for prolonged focus and detail work, as long as they can maintain the discipline of sitting still.

DESCRIPTION: This is the Gate of Determination and Commitment to a process that involves great staying power. These people can maintain a single focus and are naturally gifted at handling details. This gate is related directly to the mental gate 62 (Preponderance of The Small).

Without the 52 these people can find it hard to still themselves enough to channel their energies in a single direction.

ADVANCED KEYNOTES

Pressure Release Gate – The power to maintain the focus
Format Energy Gate – Focussed
Personality Sun Crosses – Planning, Focus, Identification
Foundation of Hexagram – 9.1 – Sensibility
Genetic Codon Group – Threonine (9,5,26,11)

Gate of Potential Depression – Restlessness –
Why can't I sit still?
Memory Network – The Power to Concentrate
Food Types – Proteins (staying power)
Other Keynotes – Gate of Restraint

 ## THE GATE OF STILLNESS –
KEEPING STILL (MOUNTAIN)

QUICK REFERENCE THEME: People with deep staying power as long as they can find the right outlet through which they can be of service.

DESCRIPTION: This gate fuels the whole Understanding Circuit with the frequency of focus and concentration. It is a Gate of Passive Tension. These people experience a kind of locked pressure to remain in one place without moving. This can sometimes be mistaken for antisocial behaviour.

With the presence of the 9 their energy can be released into one single focused stream. Without the 9, there is the potential to focus, but without the knowledge of what to focus their energy upon. A lack of focus in these people can lead to tension, restlessness and depression.

This is the so-called 'Buddha' Gate – the ability to still the physical body and senses and use energy in a focused way.

ADVANCED KEYNOTES

Pressure Gate – The pressure to concentrate
Format Energy Gate – Focussed
Foundation of Hexagram – 52.1 – Think before you speak
Personality Sun Crosses – Service, Stillness, Demands
Genetic Codon Group – Serine (58,54,53,39,52,15)

Gate of Potential Depression – Guilt –
Why am I sitting still?
Memory Network – The Fuel to Focus
Food Types – Proteins (staying power)
Other Keynotes – Gate of Passive Tension

THE CHANNEL OF RHYTHM
A DESIGN OF BEING IN THE FLOW
CIRCUIT: The Understanding Circuit
CHANNEL TYPE: Generated Channel

QUICK REFERENCE THEME: You are a very magnetic person. You pull everyone you meet into your own natural rhythm. If the world seems chaotic, it is because you are. If you are in the flow, everything you do is effortless.

WHOLE CHANNEL: These people are here to bring us into harmony with the life force and creation itself, aligning us with the deeper patterns in life. They have their own unique rhythm and can be a very magnetic presence. They can adjust their own rhythm to suit changing circumstances and are time-keepers with an innate sense of tempo and attunement to their environment. It is not possible for them to be either early or late. They are always in their own rhythm, and they automatically bring anyone in their aura into their own rhythm. When responding to life, these people are always in a wonderful flow with all life.

The 5/15 connection between two people can be challenging in intimate relationships as the two very different life rhythms are directly in conflict. The 5 needs fixed rhythms and the 15 needs changing rhythms.

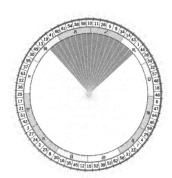

5 Quarter of Mutation
THEME: TRANSFORMATION

15 Quarter of Civilisation
THEME: FORM

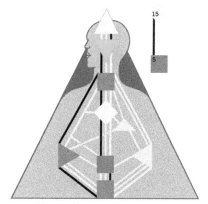

The Understanding Circuit
THE CHANNEL OF RHYTHM

THE GATE OF FIXED RHYTHMS — WAITING

QUICK REFERENCE THEME: People who need fixed rhythms and routines in life.

DESCRIPTION: This gate fixes the pattern of all life, holding all creatures and humans together in a wider universal rhythm. Out of this gate emerges a deep sense of security that comes as a result of everything following a universal flow.

This is the Gate of Habits, daily rhythm and tempo. These people have a need to follow regular rhythms in their lives. They tend to have fixed habits that they do not like to break. It can be very destabilising for them if they are forced to change their routine since their routine actually keeps them healthy.

When the 15 is present as a harmonic, this can be uncomfortable as the security of the 5's routine is disrupted.

ADVANCED KEYNOTES

Energy Control Gate – The following of a fixed pattern
Foundation of Hexagram – 5.1 – Perseverance
Personality Sun Crosses – Consciousness, Habits, Separation
Genetic Codon Group – Threonine (9,5,26,11)
Memory Network – The Power to Repeat

Dreamrave Key – Time (Earth Plane)
Design of Forms – Cross Species Gate (Plants), Gate of Habits (mammals), Fixed Collective Patterns (Birds, Reptiles, Fish), Pattern Type (single cell)
Nutritional – Fixed digestive pattern
Other Keynotes – Gate of Ritual, the Breath of Life

THE GATE OF EXTREMES — MODESTY

QUICK REFERENCE THEME: People with a need to adjust and adapt their rhythm to changing circumstances.

DESCRIPTION: These people have no fixed rhythm in life, embracing a whole spectrum of different rhythms and extremes. They thrive on diversity and need to remain constantly fluid, rather than feel fixed into any long-term pattern.

This gate represents the acceptance of the immense diversity of all forms of life, symbolised by the love of humanity. These people have an inherent magnetism because of their ability to accept without judgement the rhythms of others. This is the Gate of the "Aura" and amplifies the power and attractiveness of the magnetic monopole, thus these are magnetic people.

Without the consistency of the 5, the 15 lacks the ability to focus its rhythm and attain true mastery. These people can be uncomfortable with fixed rhythms and routines.

ADVANCED KEYNOTES

Energy Alignment Gate – Adaptation to the extremes of rhythm
Gate of the Vessel of Love – The love of humanity – The outer skin of the vessel
Foundation of Hexagram – 15.1 – Duty
Personality Sun Crosses – Vessel of Love, Extremes, Prevention
Genetic Codon Group – Serine (58,54,53,39,52,15)
Dreamrave Key – Chaos (Earth Plane)

Design of Forms – Animal magnetism – the Alpha (Mammals), Atmosphere/The Planetary aura – the diversity of patterns (Plants), Vibration diversity (Insects), Magnetic harmony (Reptiles, Birds, Fish), Rhythm/Growth rate (single cell)
Nutritional – Rhythm regulator
Memory Network – Memory flow regulator
Other Keynotes – Summer Solstice, The Big Aura, The Extremist

THE CHANNEL OF THE ALPHA
A DESIGN OF LEADERSHIP FOR 'GOOD' OR 'BAD'
CIRCUIT: The Understanding Circuit
CHANNEL TYPE: Generated Channel

QUICK REFERENCE THEME: You are designed to be picked out of the crowd one day as a true leader. The more reluctant you are to assume this status, the better a leader you will be.

WHOLE CHANNEL: These are the truest leaders, as they understand patterns and trends and are able to present them in ways that everyone can understand. They are here to lead us into the future.

These leaders have to be elected by their people. They are best reflected by modern democratic style leaders whose purpose is to represent the people rather than rule them (this is a very different type of leadership from the autocratic tribal leadership of the 45). If these people are attuned to the rhythms of those they lead, they can lead with great efficiency. If they lose touch with the needs of the collective, they can equally lead us into disaster.

These people are not necessarily formal leaders, but can also be leaders in their given field (e.g. artists, actors etc.), or they may be people who have mastered something and find themselves in positions of influence.

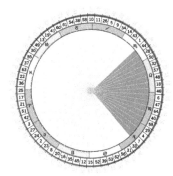

7 Quarter of Duality
THEME: RELATIONSHIPS

31 Quarter of Civilisation
THEME: FORM

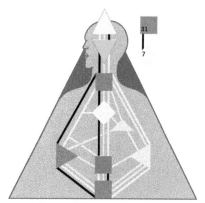

The Understanding Circuit
THE CHANNEL OF THE ALPHA

THE GATE OF THE ROLE OF THE SELF IN INTERACTION — THE ARMY

QUICK REFERENCE THEME: People with an innate impulse to lead, yet who need to be invited or elected to do so.

DESCRIPTION: This is the Gate of Leadership which is well symbolised as 'the power behind the throne'. These people do not naturally have the power of public influence, although they embody the essence of leadership (look at the line number to see what kind of leader they are: Line 1 – Authoritarian, Line 2 – Democrat, Line 3 – Anarchist, Line 4 – Abdicator, Line 5 – General, Line 6 – Administrator).

These people lead either by bringing a new rhythm to society or by destroying an old one. They have both the gift of sensing where something needs to go in order to attain its goal, and the authority to take it to that goal.

Without the 31, these are natural leaders who are not necessarily public figureheads. It is the 31 which gives them the voice and stature to reach the masses. When working together they have tremendous power to condition others (e.g: Hilary Clinton 7 and Bill Clinton 31).

ADVANCED KEYNOTES

Role Gate – Projection and logical expression of the self
Foundation of Hexagram – **7.1** – The Authoritarian
Personality Sun Crosses – Sphinx, Interaction, Masks

Genetic Codon Group – Valine (59,29,4,7)
Gate of the Sphinx – Direction towards the Future
Other keynotes – The Power behind the Throne

THE GATE OF LEADING — INFLUENCE

QUICK REFERENCE THEME: People who are best showing others how to attain future goals, rather than leading them themselves.

DESCRIPTION: These people can be very influential provided they speak with the right timing. Despite their power, the 31 cannot offer their guidance to others. They have to be elected or invited to be influential. They are figureheads that can carry us towards a new future, and when they speak of the future, people are always ready to listen. However, this is simply a Gate of Influence, without specifying whether that be good or bad.

Without the presence of the 7, the 31 may just seem like an empty voice, as they may have no sense of identification or power behind their words.

ADVANCED KEYNOTES

Expression Gate – The elected leader Voice: "I lead"
Foundation of Hexagram – **31.1** – Manifestation
Personality Sun Crosses – Unexpected, Influence, Alpha

Genetic Codon Group – Tyrosine (31,62)
Other keynotes – The Voice of Democracy, Verbal Leadership

THE CHANNEL OF ABSTRACTION
A DESIGN OF MENTAL ACTIVITY MIXED WITH CLARITY

CIRCUIT: The Sensing Circuit
CHANNEL TYPE: Projected Channel

QUICK REFERENCE THEME: Your mind can either be very inspiring for others, or very confusing for you. The trick is to only use your mind to resolve issues that do not concern you directly.

WHOLE CHANNEL: These people are here to create something new out of something old. They bring abstract thought into the world through the arts, philosophy, history and culture. They reshape the past in different ways, e.g. cultural revolutions.

The confusion these people experience at the mental level forces them to process the past in new and creative ways. They need to accept confusion as a part of their mental process, and if they are able to do so, they will always discover that things become clear in their own time.

These kinds of abstract minds cannot solve their own problems but are good at telling stories and recreating experiences that will inspire others.

64 Quarter of Duality
THEME: RELATIONSHIPS

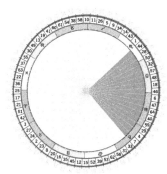

47 Quarter of Duality
THEME: RELATIONSHIPS

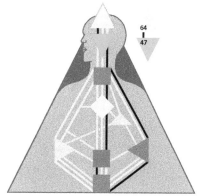

The Understanding Circuit
THE CHANNEL OF ABSTRACTION

64 THE GATE OF CONFUSION – BEFORE COMPLETION

QUICK REFERENCE THEME: People who are under constant mental pressure to make sense out of past issues or events.

DESCRIPTION: These people have to accept confusion as a part of their lives. They are visual in an abstract way – these are minds flooded by images and memories from the past. Their goal is to accept the mental pressure and wait until the images assume some kind of order. At the mental level, these people are always trying to bring resolution to their experiences.

The 64 needs the 47 to process the flood of images, otherwise it is just a confused mass of unedited rushes.

ADVANCED KEYNOTES

Pressure Gate – The pressure to resolve the past
Foundation of Hexagram – 64.1 – Conditions
Personality Sun Crosses – Consciousness, Confusion, Dominion

Genetic Codon Group – Glycine (6,64,47,40)
Awareness Stream – Stream of Sensing (Fuel of Confusion)
Other Keynotes – Gate of Madness and Dreaming (61,63,64)

47 THE GATE OF REALISATION – OPPRESSION

QUICK REFERENCE THEME: People that always look to understand life by relating it to their own personal experience.

DESCRIPTION: These people are under huge pressure to conceptualise past experience. They lay out all the images in their minds, trying to piece them together, like an artist assembling a collage. If they are patient, they can create inspiration out of confusion. Ultimately, these people are much better at resolving other people's past experiences rather than their own.

Without the 64 they are always waiting for the flash of inspiration that brings the mental pressure to a temporary end.

ADVANCED KEYNOTES

Conceptual Processing Gate – The awareness to recognise what makes sense
Foundation of Hexagram – 47.1 – Taking Stock
Personality Sun Crosses – Rulership, Oppression, Informing
Genetic Codon Group – Glycine (6,64,47,40)

Awareness Stream – Stream of Sensing (Potential to Realise)
Gate of Fear – The Fear of the futility of the Past
Gate of Anxiety – Anxiety over Confusion
Other Keynotes – Gate of Adversity, Repression

THE CHANNEL OF CURIOSITY
A DESIGN OF A SEEKER
CIRCUIT: The Sensing Circuit
CHANNEL TYPE: Projected Channel

QUICK REFERENCE THEME: You are a pure seeker, which means you are never supposed to achieve any final goal. Only when you let go of the idea of attainment altogether, can you rest and find peace in the journey itself.

WHOLE CHANNEL: These people are the great storytellers and can have a real gift for using language. They take their life experiences and fashion them into stories or anecdotes in order to get a reaction from their listeners. These ideas and experiences serve as stimulation for reflection and learning for others.

These are people who are here to seek rather than to find. It is the seeking process that is important for them, rather than the end result. They experience an endless curiosity for new ideas, and have to learn that the ideas they have are never for them, but can always be useful and stimulating for others. They need to realise that the abstract mind cannot solve its own problems.

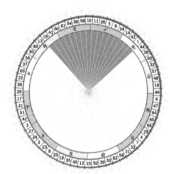

11 Quarter of Mutation
THEME: TRANSFORMATION

56 Quarter of Civilisation
THEME: FORM

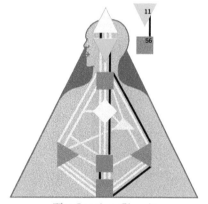

The Sensing Circuit
THE CHANNEL OF CURIOSITY

11 THE GATE OF IDEAS — PEACE

QUICK REFERENCE THEME: People whose minds are a continual font of changing ideas, most of which are never intended to manifest.

DESCRIPTION: These people experience constant streams of ideas, many of which may never be realised and most of which are intended to be shared with others rather than applied to oneself. They love stimulation and also need to stimulate others in the sharing of their ideas.

This gate puts together all the pieces that were gathered in the 64/47 and weaves them into a specific shape. Depending on the way in which we process the past, the 11 forms our basic beliefs and belief systems. The left eye represents our visual memory, and thus we need time in order to see the full picture. It expresses ideas rather than facts.

Without the 56, these are ideas and/or ideals waiting for the right moment to be expressed.

ADVANCED KEYNOTES

Conceptual Crystallisation Gate – The transformation of a resolution into an idea – Visual memory (the left eye)
Foundation of Hexagram – 11.1 – Attunement
Personality Sun Crosses – Eden, Ideas, Education
Genetic Codon Group – Threonine (11,26,5,9)

Awareness Stream – Stream of Sensing (Possibility of Ideas)
Gate of Fear – The Fear of Emptiness/Darkness
Gate of Anxiety – Anxiety over Stimulation
Memory network – Visual memory
Other Keynotes – Gate of White Magick, Ideals

56 THE GATE OF STIMULATION — THE WANDERER

QUICK REFERENCE THEME: People who use their own past experiences in order to illustrate their concepts and stimulate others.

DESCRIPTION: This is the Gate of The Storyteller. These people spin a yarn out of the ideas gathered in the 11. They are really only interested in getting an emotional reaction from their listeners. They are not interested in proof, fact or detail like the 62. They love to use their own experience in order to make a point.

They are hungry for new ideas to express, which come from the 11. Thus without the 11, they have a gift for using other people's ideas in order to get attention. They have to wait to be invited otherwise their timing is never correct.

ADVANCED KEYNOTES

Conceptual Expression Gate – Transforms visualisation into language
Voice – I believe
Foundation of Hexagram – 56.1 – Quality
Personality Sun Crosses – Laws, Stimulation, Distraction

Genetic Codon Group – Stop Codon Group (56,12,33)
Awareness Stream – Stream of Sensing (Expression of Belief)
Memory Network – Memory projection (I believe)
Other Keynotes – Gate of Travelling, Storytelling

35 / 36 THE CHANNEL OF TRANSITORINESS
A DESIGN OF BEING A 'JACK OF ALL TRADES'
CIRCUIT: The Sensing Circuit (Creative Channel)
CHANNEL TYPE: Manifested Channel

QUICK REFERENCE THEME: Yours is a life rich in experience, though poor in meeting the expectations of your own mind or of others. Your deepest talent is for adventure. Your goal – the wisdom that nothing lasts.

SEXUALITY KEYNOTE: The Channel of Sexual Talent.

WHOLE CHANNEL: These people are driven to constantly seek out new experiences in life. Theirs is a journey of gathering wisdom through experience. The experiences they have are all part of a wider plan that eventually can give them great depth. However, their personal lives can often seem to pay the price if they do not understand how they operate.

Since this is the Creative Channel of the Sensing Circuit, these people have a talent for adventure. They are driven by the genetic hunger for change. They move through one experience after another for the wisdom rather than the result of the experience. As they mature, they become more and more creative as they share their experiences, both good and bad, with others. They can be wonderful storytellers as they have so many fascinating experiences.

A very sexual channel, this is the channel of 'I've been there, done that!'. The dilemma of these people is that no experience is really personal, because they are driven by a genetic need to experience something new. This is sex that is all about the experience rather than the person, which can be a big disappointment when the experience is over. The secret for such people is to surrender all their expectations and simply enjoy the experience, or not!

These people must wait to be emotionally clear. If they do not wait and things go wrong, they can get trapped in a repetitive loop of doing it again and again. This is a Manifesting Channel, which means that these people can also be deeply volatile when their experiences turn out differently from their expectations.

35 Quarter of Civilisation
THEME: FORM

36 Quarter of Initiation
THEME: MIND

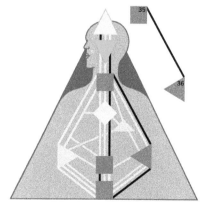

The Sensing Circuit
THE CHANNEL OF TRANSITORINESS

35 THE GATE OF CHANGE – PROGRESS

QUICK REFERENCE THEME: People who sample many different things in life in order to learn from them.

DESCRIPTION: These are people who are always ready to try a new experience, often without giving a thought to the repercussions. This is the Gate of Hunger for Something New. Once an experience has been tried, the hunger is fulfilled for a short while until a new cycle arrives and once again the hunger returns. These are people who can thus be multi-talented, hence the keynote for this channel – a 'jack of all trades'.

Because this is the Gate of being Empty and/or Full, these people are easily bored when nothing is happening. They are always seeking the emotional rush of diving into the 36. If they do not wait before they leap into something new, crisis is usually the result.

The 35/36 is a very strong magnetic connection sexually, being the Channel of Sexual Talent. The 35 looks to the 36 because it represents an unknown experience and is thus excited at the prospect of trying something new. However, the frequent result of such connections is disappointment, since the drive to try something new disappears as soon as it has been fulfilled. The secret is for these people to wait to be clear first.

ADVANCED KEYNOTES

Expression Gate – Manifestation of new experiences
Voice – I feel (like a change)
Foundation of Hexagram – 35.1 – Humility
Personality Sun Crosses – Consciousness, Experience, Separation
Genetic Codon Group – Tryptophan (35)
Awareness Stream – Stream of Feeling (Expression of change)

Gate of Sexuality (Emotional) – Gate of Sexual boredom, a design of Experience
Nutritional – Fuel gauge for hunger (fullness)
Other keynotes – Gate of Satiation ('been there, done that'), a 'Jack of All Trades'.

36 THE GATE OF CRISIS – THE DARKENING OF THE LIGHT

QUICK REFERENCE THEME: People who are here to grow through profound emotional experience.

DESCRIPTION: This is the Gate of Emotional Turbulence, which usually occurs once the desires of the 30 are expressed. These people are here to learn to handle emotional experiences and to find clarity by going through all kinds of emotional challenges – both the highs and lows are here to be moved through cycles during which inexperience is transformed into experience. They learn through constant change, which can prove to be both very exciting or deeply overwhelming and destabilising.

These are people with an untapped depth of feelings that are always waiting for someone to trigger them. They need the 35 in order to meet the new experience.

ADVANCED KEYNOTES

Emotional Awareness Gate (Potential) – The power to Feel
Foundation of Hexagram – 36.1 – Resistance
Personality Sun Crosses – Eden, Crisis, Plane
Genetic Codon Group – Proline (37,63,22,36)
Awareness Stream – Stream of Feeling (Possibility of Crisis)

Gate of Sexuality (Emotional) – Gate of Sexual Crisis, a design of Inexperience
Gate of Fear – The Fear of Emotional Inadequacy
Gate of Nervousness – Nervousness over expectations
Nutritional – Wave of Hunger
Other keynotes – Gate of Juiciness, 'Fucking'

THE CHANNEL OF RECOGNITION
A DESIGN OF FOCUSED ENERGY (FEELINGS)
CIRCUIT: The Sensing Circuit
CHANNEL TYPE: Projected Channel

QUICK REFERENCE THEME: You are one of life's great dreamers. You have only 2 lessons to learn in life: 1) Don't try and make your dreams come true. 2) Don't expect any of your desires to bring you lasting peace. True peace is simply to enjoy the dreams themselves.

SEXUALITY KEYNOTE: The Channel of Desire.

WHOLE CHANNEL: These people are here to gain wisdom through exploring all kinds of feelings. They are natural dreamers, and yet so many of their dreams are never even supposed to come true. Despite this, they have a profound ability to stir the feelings of others through the dreams and wishes that they share.

Being a direct connection between the Solar Plexus and the Root Centres, this channel brings an emotional pressure often experienced as a restlessness or nervousness (particularly when split off from other definitions). This channel is a mirror of the 18/58. Whereas the Channel of Judgement endlessly wants to correct in order to improve, the 41/30 endlessly yearns to feel in order to learn.

These people often need to learn patience and composure. They have to play hard to get in terms of making decisions, allowing themselves to move through their emotional wave from hope to pain in order to finally see which of their desires are correct.

41 Quarter of Mutation
THEME: TRANSFORMATION

30 Quarter of Initiation
THEME: MIND

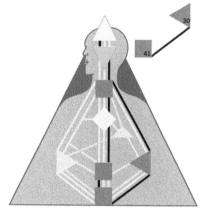

The Sensing Circuit
THE CHANNEL OF RECOGNITION

41 THE GATE OF CONTRACTION – DECREASE

QUICK REFERENCE THEME: People driven by the incessant urge to experience a new feeling.

DESCRIPTION: This is the Gate of Fantasy – these people constantly fantasise about having new experiences. This gate represents an impulse to do something new – it is the pressure to seek experience through feeling, fantasy, excitement or a thirst for destiny.

The pressure of this gate is often experienced as a feeling of restlessness, as though something new is beginning, but without the 30th gate, it cannot crystalise to become a specific desire. These people can therefore experience a confusion of feelings (similar to the 64th gate who experience a confusion of thoughts).

Without the 30, these people know they want change, but they don't know what kind of change.

ADVANCED KEYNOTES

Pressure Gate – The pressure to have a new experience
Foundation of Hexagram – 41.1 – Reasonableness
Personality Sun Crosses – Unexpected, Fantasy, Alpha
Genetic Codon Group – Methonine – Start codon (41)
Awareness Stream – Stream of Feeling (Fuel of Fantasy)

Gate of Love – The Love of Dreams
Gate of Sexuality (Emotional) – Gate of Sexual Hunger, a design of Fantasy
Nutritional – Fuel gauge for hunger (Emptiness)
Other keynotes – Gate of Fantasy

30 THE GATE OF FEELINGS – THE CLINGING FIRE

QUICK REFERENCE THEME: People who can never be free from desires.

DESCRIPTION: This is the Gate of Desire and it is the source of all our emotional aches and yearnings. These people may not know what their longing is for, but they are driven to want to try all kinds of new things, the result of which may or may not be the gaining of wisdom. The 41 narrows down the emotional field by focussing on a single fantasy or desire at a time.

This is also the Gate of the Fates. Given the power that desire has over human beings, the greatest lesson these people can learn is not to take experiences personally. As long as they are able to enter into new situations from a clear emotional space, whatever they learn will be correct for them, even if it doesn't meet their expectations.

These people can never afford to give way to their expectations about what their desires will bring them.

ADVANCED KEYNOTES

Awareness Processing Gate – The potential of recognising a feeling
Foundation of Hexagram – 30.1 – Composure
Personality Sun Crosses – Contagion, Fates, Industry
Genetic Codon Group – Glutamine (13,30)
Awareness Stream – Stream of Feeling (Fuel of Fantasy)

Gate of Fear – The Fear of Fate
Gate of Nervousness – Nervousness over Feelings
Gate of Sexuality (Emotional) – Gate of Sexual feelings, a design of Yearning
Nutritional – Hunger Recognition
Other keynotes – Gate of the Fates, Desire

THE CHANNEL OF MATURATION
A DESIGN OF BALANCED DEVELOPMENT (CYCLIC)
CIRCUIT: The Sensing Circuit
CHANNEL TYPE: Generated Channel

QUICK REFERENCE THEME: Every time you begin something new, be very cautious. Once you have committed yourself to an endeavour, you have a genetic imperative to complete it. If you do not follow it to its natural conclusion, you will only meet the same problem again later in another form.

WHOLE CHANNEL: These people live lives dominated by repeating cycles that bring them gradually and steadily to a state of maturity and wisdom. They are here to embody the wisdom that all life is a journey that never ends. They are not here to be goal oriented, but rather to learn to appreciate all the rich experiences of the journey itself. Such people can become deeply attuned to the cycles of life, planetary cycles, body cycles, historical cycles etc, as well as having a deep affinity with the past.

Whatever these people begin in life must be finished. All projects, relationships and experiences must therefore be entered into clearly and correctly, otherwise these people find that they either have to wait for a cycle to naturally end (usually 7 years), or they jump out prematurely and face the same pattern all over again in a different experience.

The cyclical format energy governs the whole of the Sensing Circuit and this channel will condition all other definitions in the Bodygraph to operate according to a cyclic process.

53 Quarter of Civilisation
THEME: FORM

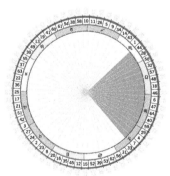

42 Quarter of Initiation
THEME: MIND

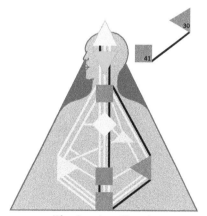

The Sensing Circuit
THE CHANNEL OF MATURATION

53 THE GATE OF BEGINNINGS – DEVELOPMENT

QUICK REFERENCE THEME: People under constant pressure to begin something new.

DESCRIPTION: These are people that can feel deeply trapped and bored when stuck facing the same old situations. As long as they begin things according to their design, it is not necessary for them to finish them. These are people that can happily leave books unfinished, meals uneaten etc.

Without the 42, they may begin projects that are never finished, or they feel compelled to finish projects that they do not want to finish themselves.

ADVANCED KEYNOTES

Pressure Gate – Cyclic energy, pressure to begin a new cycle
Format Energy Gate – Cycles
Foundation of Hexagram – 53.1 – Accumulation
Personality Sun Crosses – Penetration, Beginnings, Cycles
Genetic Codon Group – Serine (58,54,53,39,52,15)
Gate of Potential Depression – Not being able to finish anything/being trapped

Dreamrave Key – Flight (Demon Realm)
Design of Forms – Mammalian Vitality
Nutritional – Initiator of eating cycle
Food Type – Fats/Carbohydrates
Other Keynotes – Gate of Freedom

42 THE GATE OF GROWTH – INCREASE

QUICK REFERENCE THEME: People with an imperative to always finish what they have begun.

DESCRIPTION: These people are under tremendous pressure to finish everything they begin, and have the power and commitment to follow any endeavour all the way through to the end. Being people who like to see things through to the end, they are often uncomfortable with new beginnings and the inevitable difficulties that accompany them.

These people can often feel as if they are stuck in cycles that never seem to end, such as childhood patterns or recurring themes in their relationships. To avoid this, they always need to allow things to come to a natural conclusion, rather than force a premature ending.

They need the energy of the 53 to provide the initiating spark. Only then can they apply their staying power to a process.

ADVANCED KEYNOTES

Pressure Release Gate – The energy to finish the cycle
Format Energy Gate – Cycles
Foundation of Hexagram – 42.1 – Diversification
Personality Sun Crosses – Maya, Completion, Limitation
Genetic Codon Group – Leucine (42,3,27,24,20,23)
Gate of Potential Depression – Not being able to begin something new

Dreamrave Key – Dying (Demon Realm)
Design of Forms – Power to mature through cycles
Nutritional – Cycle Regulator
Food Type – Fats/Carbohydrates
Other Keynotes – Gate of Quitting, Closure

THE CHANNEL OF DISCOVERY
A DESIGN OF SUCCEEDING WHERE OTHERS FAIL
CIRCUIT: The Sensing Circuit
CHANNEL TYPE: Generated Channel

QUICK REFERENCE THEME: Once you are clear about making a commitment, you have to totally abandon yourself to it, releasing all expectations about its outcome. In this way, you will learn there is no such thing as failure or success, but only continual discovery.

WHOLE CHANNEL: These people are here to lose themselves in their experiences until their experiences come to an end. If they are only half committed, they will learn nothing. This is about being in the Now of the experience of being alive. For these people, the true meaning of any experience can only be known at the end, thus they have to let go of all expectations.

These people must learn to surrender to the cyclical nature of their lives and allow the potential of unexpected discovery. If they do not make correct and clear commitments then their bodies will suffer from the stress of constant crisis, disappointment or upheaval.

In this channel the abstract process finds promise or chaos – this is the design of succeeding where others fail, or failing where others succeed.

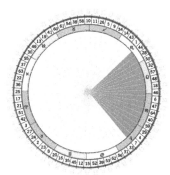

29 Quarter of Duality
THEME: RELATIONSHIPS

46 Quarter of Duality
THEME: RELATIONSHIPS

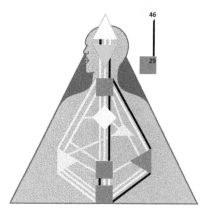

The Sensing Circuit
THE CHANNEL OF DISCOVERY

THE GATE OF SAYING 'YES' — THE ABYSMAL

QUICK REFERENCE THEME: People with the power to commit themselves to a process without the need to know where it will take them.

DESCRIPTION: A very powerful gate, this is the Gate of Commitment and saying 'Yes' to life. When the Sacral Centre responds from this gate, it is saying 'yes' to a whole new cycle. These people must be wary of over-committing their energies out of their conditioning. Ideally, they must wait to be asked in order to make a correct commitment in life.

They are here to learn to distinguish between what is worth committing to and what is not. The Sacral "Yes" provides the fuel to persevere despite circumstances. These people must trust their 'Yes', entering into a new experience with no preconceived notion of what it might bring them.

The 46 brings them the love of the experience – the juiciness of simply doing something for the sake of doing it. Without the 46, the 29 is ready to work, but has no idea what it is working towards.

ADVANCED KEYNOTES

Energy Control Gate – Persistence – The Sacral "Yes"
Foundation of Hexagram – 29.1 – The Draftee
Personality Sun Crosses – Contagion, Commitment, Industry

Genetic Codon Group – Valine (59,29,4,7)
Other Keynotes – Gate of Slavery, Commitment

 # THE GATE OF DETERMINATION — PUSHING UPWARD

QUICK REFERENCE THEME: People who are always in the right place at the right time when they let go of their expectations.

DESCRIPTION: This gate is about loving the perfection of every experience, no matter how unpleasant the experience may be. For people with this gate every experience is right and no feeling should be escaped.

This is the Gate of Sensuality, of love of the body and the honouring of the flesh as our temple. This gate represents the magic of trusting in our natural responses to take us through life in the perfect timing.

Without the 29, the 46 may know the right timing, but lacks the commitment to either begin or stay with their process.

ADVANCED KEYNOTES

Energy Alignment Gate – Determination to follow through with their commitment
Gate of the Vessel of Love – The love of the body – The inner body of the vessel
Foundation of Hexagram – 46.1 – Being discovered

Personality Sun Crosses – Vessel of Love, Serendipity, Healing
Genetic Codon Group – Alanine (57,48,18,46)
Other Keynotes – Gate of Serendipity, Flesh, Autumn equinox

13 33 THE CHANNEL OF THE PRODIGAL
A DESIGN OF A WITNESS
CIRCUIT: The Sensing Circuit
CHANNEL TYPE: Projected Channel

QUICK REFERENCE THEME: Every cycle of experience in your life will make sense in the end. This is what you are here to learn over and over again. The deeper you experience this insight, the more patient and relaxed you will become with the way things are going in the now.

WHOLE CHANNEL: These people are here to pass on the wisdom of individual experience to others. Their emphasis in life is to learn from hindsight and pass on what they have learned so that others do not have to make the same mistakes.

For these people the past is always important. Whether they are historians, comedians or politicians these people are natural record keepers – this can be seen in any number of things, from keeping photo albums to accounts or diaries.

People with this channel often hear and know more than they let on. They can have a profound memory for certain information. In an organisation, these are the people to ask if you need to know what is going on beneath the surface. Because of these gifts, they are often sought out as leaders.

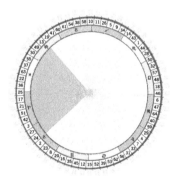

13 Quarter of Initiation
THEME: MIND

33 Quarter of Civilisation
THEME: FORM

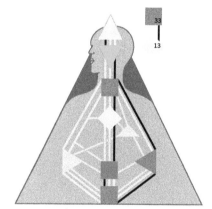

The Sensing Circuit
THE CHANNEL OF THE PRODIGAL

13 THE GATE OF THE LISTENER — THE FELLOWSHIP OF MAN

QUICK REFERENCE THEME: People who are natural listeners.

DESCRIPTION: These people often get to hear what others do not. If they wait, they will soon see that they are always hearing other people's secrets. They are natural recorders of experience and history as they attract the sharing of experiences from others. Because of these gifts, these people often know more than those around them even though they do not necessarily share this.

This gate is a point of completion in the Sensing Circuit, where the memory of all cycles of experience are held. These people need the 33's in order to remember and release what they have heard and taken in, otherwise the secrets may never emerge. Without a 33, they will keep their secrets to themselves.

ADVANCED KEYNOTES

Role Gate – Reflection, the recording of the past
Foundation of Hexagram – 13.1 – Empathy
Personality Sun Crosses – Sphinx, Listening, Masks
Genetic Codon Group – Glutamine (13,30)

Gate of the Sphinx – Direction from the Past
Memory Network – Memory collection
Other keynotes – The Hearer of Secrets

33 THE GATE OF PRIVACY — RETREAT

QUICK REFERENCE THEME: People who need regular time alone in order to reflect on the past.

DESCRIPTION: These people have the power to express the experiences of the Sensing Circuit. However, they need to withdraw into their privacy in order to process their experiences. They are symbolised by the archetype of the wise story-teller – a person who can always share all sides of an experience, as well as show us what we might learn from it.

The storyteller here is very different from the 56, which is more about the stirring up of other's emotions. The purpose of the 33 is to reveal the underlying secrets or lessons behind any experience.

These people can be powerful orators, writers and teachers. By dint of their design, they have to understand that they are supposed to become more influential as they get older, and mature their wisdom through many cycles.

Without the 13, the 33 can always share its experiences, but it lacks the depth to learn from them.

ADVANCED KEYNOTES

Abstract Expression Gate – Recounting of past experience
Voice – I remember
Foundation of Hexagram – 33.1 – Avoidance
Personality Sun Crosses – Four Ways, Retreat, Refinement

Genetic Codon Group – Stop Codon Group (33,12,56)
Gate of Aloneness – (33,12,40)
Memory Network – Memory expression
Other keynotes – Gate of Revelation, Storyteller, Historian

54 / 32 THE CHANNEL OF TRANSFORMATION
A DESIGN OF BEING DRIVEN

CIRCUIT: The Ego Circuit
CHANNEL TYPE: Projected Channel

QUICK REFERENCE THEME: You have within you the capacity and drive to attain any distant goal. However, you cannot get to your goal without the correct allies in life to support you. Ideally, you need to wait for your allies to recognise you for your momentous drive, rather than you trying to find them.

SEXUALITY KEYNOTE: The Channel of Encouragement.

WHOLE CHANNEL: These people are here to transform raw energy into something that endures. It is about transforming hard work into material success. These people have the sensitivity to balance vigour with restraint, creating any enterprise or business that can always sustain itself.

This channel is about time, money, value, business and bargaining. These people can always evaluate whether the time and effort spent is worth the money earned. Because of this, these people know how to recognise someone else's worth as well as their own and they are always willing to bargain with others to get their own and others needs met.

These people have a deep need to be materially successful and are willing to work very hard for recognition. Ideally, they are looking to move up in the hierarchy, and this usually happens through them making the correct contacts. When these people do not value themselves or their place in the community properly, they can become workaholics.

54 Quarter of Mutation
THEME: TRANSFORMATION

32 Quarter of Duality
THEME: RELATIONSHIPS

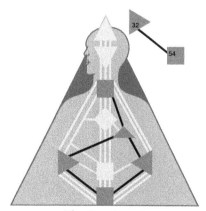

The Ego Circuit
THE CHANNEL OF TRANSFORMATION

THE GATE OF AMBITION –
THE MARRYING MAIDEN

QUICK REFERENCE THEME: People with a limitless drive to be materially successful.

DESCRIPTION: This gate represents the drive to move up the social ladder and attain higher status. It also represents material ambition and the drive to make money. These people are the driving forces within the community, and in particular, the business community.

The archetype of this gate is the concubine who rises up in the hierarchy to finally become the empress. These people are always trying in someway to catch the attention of someone higher up in the hierarchy. This also applies at a mystical level.

On its own, the 54 is a blind urge to achieve a certain end. It needs the conservatism and instinct of the 32 to channel its ambitious drive into something lasting and of value.

ADVANCED KEYNOTES

Pressure Gate – The drive to move up the hierarchy
Foundation of Hexagram – 54.1 – Influence
Personality Sun Crosses – Penetration, Ambition, Cycles
Genetic Codon Group – Serine (58,54,53,39,52,15)
Awareness Stream – Stream of Instinct (Fuel of Ambition)
Gate of Sexuality (Caring) – Gate of Caring needs, a design of Familiarity

Memory Network – The drive to expand memory
Nutritional – Liquid Production
Other keynotes – The Concubine, Enlightenment/ Endarkenment, The Worker

THE GATE OF CONTINUITY – DURATION

QUICK REFERENCE THEME: People with an in-born instinct for the true value of anything or anyone.

DESCRIPTION: Archetypally, this gate represents the financial manager of the entrepreneurial 54. These people have a nose for the value of both things and people. They are also very conservative by nature, knowing that restraint ensures continuity and long term success.

The fear of this gate is the fear of failure, which is what makes these people so conservative. However, it is this conservatism that ensures continuity and health, not only for the individual, but the community or business.

The 32 potentially knows what can or cannot be transformed successfully and acts as the brake on the drive of the 54. The 32 always needs the driving spark from the 54 and without it the 32 asks: "Will I ever have the drive or ambition?".

ADVANCED KEYNOTES

Awareness Refining Gate – Awareness of what is of value and can be transformed
Foundation of Hexagram – 32.1 – Conservation
Personality Sun Crosses – Maya, Conservation, Limitation
Genetic Codon Group – Aspartic Acid (28,32)
Awareness Stream – Stream of Instinct (Potential to Transform)
Gate of Fear – The Fear of Failure

Gate of Sexuality (Caring) – Gate of Caring requirements, a design of demanding Respect or not
Memory Network – Instinct – Awareness of what is essential to remember
Nutritional – Liquid Regulator
Other keynotes – The Financial Manager, Conservativeness, Apprenticeship

44 / 26 THE CHANNEL OF SURRENDER
A DESIGN OF A TRANSMITTER

CIRCUIT: The Ego Circuit (Creative Channel)
CHANNEL TYPE: Projected Channel

QUICK REFERENCE THEME: Your gift is for working with people. You have an instinct for knowing how to present anything to anyone in such a way so that you and your message are recognised. Your lesson in life is to wait until your market finds you, rather than you trying to sell yourself for recognition.

SEXUALITY KEYNOTE: The Channel of Manipulation.

WHOLE CHANNEL: These people are here to use their instincts in order to sell a message, product or truth. Their gift is to know exactly how to adapt their expression to a specific person or group in order to attain their goal.

As part of the Creative Channel of the Ego Circuit, this gate represents the creative art of enterprise; of making contact with the community in order to manipulate them into buying something. These people have a gift for relaying information to others for their own ends, and because they are so splenic, they can instinctively and spontaneously adjust their position to meet any changing market or situation. Such people can be wonderful film makers, advertisers, salesmen etc.

These people are always looking to improve their work/rest ratio – i.e. their aim is to be paid more for doing less, whilst remaining just as effective.

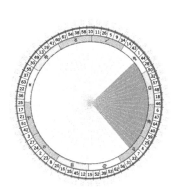

44 Quarter of Duality
THEME: RELATIONSHIPS

26 Quarter of Mutation
THEME: TRANSFORMATION

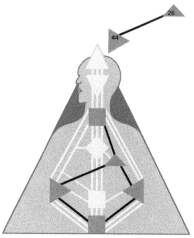

The Ego Circuit
THE CHANNEL OF SURRENDER

44 THE GATE OF ALERTNESS — COMING TO MEET

QUICK REFERENCE THEME: People with an instinctive knowledge of the capabilities of others.

DESCRIPTION: Represented by the archetype of the Personnel Manager, these people have a genius for sensing the gifts/skills and potentials of others. They have a 'nose' for people and can always rely on their hunches (if the spleen is defined).

This is the Gate of Instinctive Memory where past experiences are held within the cellular memory of the body. Thus these people are designed to operate out of an instinctive alertness based on their successes and/or failures in the past. This fear of the past being repeated is a human survival mechanism that protects not only the individual but the community that they are a part of.

The 44 needs to trade their instinct with the 26, which represents the willpower to actually handle people effectively. Without the 26, the 44 remains only an instinct for knowing about people without the ability to manage them.

ADVANCED KEYNOTES

Awareness Manipulation Gate – Instinctive awareness rooted in the power of memory (Gate of the nose)
Foundation of Hexagram – 44.1 – Conditions
Personality Sun Crosses – Four Ways, Alertness, Incarnation
Genetic Codon Group – Glutamic Acid (44,50)
Awareness Stream – Stream of Instinct (Possibility of being alert)
Gate of Love – The Love of Talent

Gate of Fear – The Fear of the Past
Gate of Sexuality (Caring) – Gate of Instinct for Caring, a design of Spontaneous Affection
Design of Forms – Alertness – The fear of being eaten (birds, reptiles, fish)
Memory Network – Cellular Memory – Storage
Nutritional – Osmatic Regulator – Cellular memory
Other keynotes – Capitalist, Entrepreneur, Cold-bloodedness

26 THE GATE OF THE EGOIST — THE TAMING POWER OF THE GREAT

QUICK REFERENCE THEME: People whose goal is to attain maximum reward for minimum output.

DESCRIPTION: Represented by the archetype of the salesperson, these people can take something that is only a raw potential and twist it around in their fingers to transform it into something marketable. This is the Gate of the Trickster, who has the confidence to manipulate any situation to their own advantage (sometimes they get caught!).

As an Ego Gate, these people naturally demand that they are rewarded for their skills. Like the 54, they want to rise up in the hierarchy, but their ultimate goal is to get to a position where they don't have to work at all.

The 26 has tremendous strength as a survivor, being able to find shortcuts in and out of most situations. However, without the 44, they have no awareness and/or people skills. They may have the presence and skill to transmit something but without the 44, they don't know to whom, when or where.

ADVANCED KEYNOTES

Ego Tempering Gate – The strength to apply memory (Thymus Gland)
Foundation of Hexagram – 26.1 – A bird in the hand
Personality Sun Crosses – Rulership, Trickster, Confrontation
Genetic Codon Group – Threonine (9,5,26,11)
Awareness Stream – Stream of Instinct (Expression of manipulation)

Gate of Sexuality (Caring) – Gate of Caring Denial, a design of Exaggeration or not
Design of Forms – Birds, reptiles, fish connection to humans
Memory Network – Power to control memory
Nutritional – Memory application
Other keynotes – Gate of Warm-bloodedness, Lying, Manipulation, Marketing, Trickster

19/49 THE CHANNEL OF SYNTHESIS
A DESIGN OF SENSITIVITY

CIRCUIT: The Ego Circuit
CHANNEL TYPE: Projected Channel

QUICK REFERENCE THEME: Your life is a constant lesson in sensitivity – to balance your own needs with those around you whilst holding fast to your own principles. Your potential gift is to be recognised as someone who can always balance practicality and fairness.

MYSTICAL CHANNEL KEYNOTE: The Channel of Animism (The Harvest and The Slaughter), the Channel of Communal Ritual, a design of Psychic Potential through Sensitivity.

SEXUALITY KEYNOTE: The Channel of the Bride and Groom.

WHOLE CHANNEL: It is in this channel that the correct strategy is laid down for entering into any kind of bond or contract with another person. These people are here to learn to be sensitive and to balance their own needs with the needs of others. They will put a lot of effort into a bond and they can be acutely sensitive or insensitive, depending on the emotional wave.

This is an emotional Projected Channel, which means that ideally these people have to be recognised by others before entering into their relationships. They must allow time and space for a natural courtship to develop so they can be emotionally clear before making any commitment.

As the root of the Stream of Touch, people with this channel demand close contact with others. Depending on whether the emotional wave is up or down, they can want to hug or want to hit.

This channel is rooted in food, environment and community. Such people need to eat together with others regularly. Food is of great importance to them.

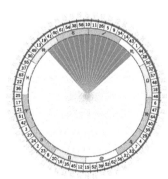

19 Quarter of Mutation
THEME: TRANSFORMATION

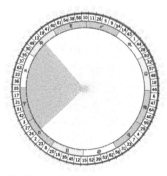

49 Quarter of Initiation
THEME: MIND

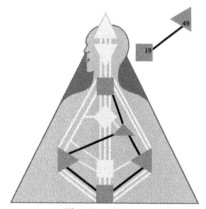

The Ego Circuit
THE CHANNEL OF SYNTHESIS

THE GATE OF NEED — APPROACH

QUICK REFERENCE THEME: People whose material and emotional needs require successful interaction with others.

DESCRIPTION: Through this gate there is a continual pressure on others to bring awareness to the needs of the immediate environment or group. Through the pressure of their design, these people always ensure that basic needs are met, in particular food, shelter and sex. People with the 19 always needs to have a full refrigerator, a place to call home and people to communicate with.

The role of these people is to flirt with others in order to see if their needs can be met. If the other person's principles (the 49) agree with their needs, they can potentially make a bargain together. Without a clear deal with the 49, the 19 knows what it needs but doesn't know how to get it.

This gate also brings a need and a potential gift for touch, as well as a potential gift for connecting with animals and nature.

ADVANCED KEYNOTES

Pressure Gate – The pressure to meet one's material needs
Foundation of Hexagram – 19.1 – Interdependence
Personality Sun Crosses – Four Ways, Need, Refinement
Genetic Codon Group – Isoleucine (61,60,19)
Awareness Stream – Stream of Sensitivity (Fuel of need)
Gate of Sexuality (Emotional) – Gate of needing sexual resources, a design of Flirtation
Design of Forms – Cross Species Gate – The drive to find food (mammals)

Dreamrave Key – Portal/Bridge – Environments (Demon Realm)
Mystical Gate – The root of animism and the energy to experience magic in nature
Nutritional – Need for Liquid Access/Food Access
Other keynotes – Gate of Neediness, Flirting, Touch, Territory

THE GATE OF REJECTION — REVOLUTION

QUICK REFERENCE THEME: People whose principles may either cause them to reject or be rejected.

DESCRIPTION: This is the gate where the principles of any relationship are established. The 49 has a need to be obeyed – if the principles of the 49 are not accepted they will reject the other person, hence this is the Gate of Divorce and Revolution.

These can be very sensitive or very insensitive people – their question is always: 'who will stand by my side and support my principles?'. Because their principles are governed by the ups and downs of the emotional wave, these people have to stay in constant communication with their loved ones in order to maintain clarity in their relationships.

They need the material resources of the 19 because otherwise they cannot necessarily maintain their principles. This gate carries a potential sensitivity or insensitivity to animals – it is the 'Gate of the Breeder or the Butcher'.

ADVANCED KEYNOTES

Awareness Processing Gate – Awareness of who and what is needed
Foundation of Hexagram – 49.1 – The law of necessity
Personality Sun Crosses – Explanation, Principles, Revolution
Genetic Codon Group – Histidine (49,55)
Awareness Stream – Stream of Sensitivity (Potential of Rejection)
Gate of Fear – The Fear of the unpredictability of Nature (The Fear of God)

Gate of Nervousness – Nervousness over Support
Gate of Sexuality (Emotional) – Gate of sexual principles, a design of Demanding Obedience
Design of Forms – Human emotional connection to mammals – the breeder/cultivator
Mystical Gate – The potential to both sacrifice and be sacrificed
Nutritional – Food Discrimination
Other keynotes – Gate of Principles, The Butcher, Killing, Violence, Revolution

$\frac{37}{40}$ THE CHANNEL OF COMMUNITY
DESIGN OF A PART SEEKING A WHOLE
CIRCUIT: The Ego Circuit
CHANNEL TYPE: Projected Channel

QUICK REFERENCE THEME: The purpose of your life is to discover where you belong in the grand scheme of things and then to live that out. Instead of trying to figure out where you fit in, wait to see which people or communities invite you in.

MYSTICAL CHANNEL KEYNOTE: The Glorious and the Profane, the Channel of Tribal Spirituality.

SEXUALITY KEYNOTE: The Channel of the Marriage Contract.

WHOLE CHANNEL: This channel represents the marriage contract and the family and is the foundation of any community. It is all about finding the right allies to bond with in order to create harmony in the community.

These people need to see that all their relationships in life have to be based on the principle of fairness. If the bargains they make with their loved ones or colleagues are not maintained in a clear and open way the bond will break down. These people have to keep a natural balance in all the aspects of their lives i.e. the practical provision of food, a regular sex life, time off for pleasure and a balanced working life.

People with this channel always want to know where and how they fit into the community, and on a mystical level, where they fit into the bigger picture – i.e. what their true purpose is.

Like the 19/49, this channel is rooted in touch, which means that these people need to become friends with those they do business with. They need to have direct contact with others rather than for example, telephone contact. They should never enter into any deal with someone they have not physically met.

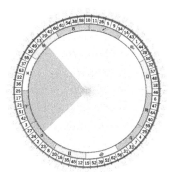
37 Quarter of Initiation
THEME: MIND

40 Quarter of Duality
THEME: RELATIONSHIPS

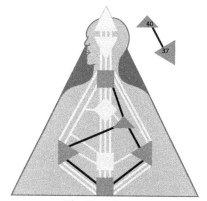
The Ego Circuit
THE CHANNEL OF COMMUNITY

37 THE GATE OF FRIENDSHIP – THE FAMILY

QUICK REFERENCE THEME: People who need recognition through family or community.

DESCRIPTION: These people actually hold the family or community together. Through their friendly nature they ensure that harmony is maintained within our communities and families. They are natural nurturers.

People with this gate always need their friendships to be built upon some sort of bargain. There are many types of bargains, but this can be as simple as one person working while the other looks after the children. Because these people constantly follow the emotional wave, they also have to constantly adjust the bargain between themselves and others. As long as this dynamic is upheld they can be very loyal people.

The 37 represents the distributor within the family, whilst the 40 represents the provider, thus these two themes are deeply reliant upon a clear bargain.

ADVANCED KEYNOTES

Awareness Manipulation Gate – Awareness of who will provide what is needed
Foundation of Hexagram – 37.1 – The Mother/Father
Personality Sun Crosses – Planning, Bargains, Migration
Genetic Codon Group – Proline (37,63,22,36)
Awareness Stream – Stream of Sensitivity (Possibility of Friendship)
Gate of Fear – The Fear of not maintaining Traditions

Gate of Nervousness – Nervousness over promises
Gate of Sexuality (Emotional) – Gate of sexual affection, a design of Cuddling
Mystical Gate – The path of Worship and the hope of being touched by God
Nutritional – The Gate of the Mouth
Other keynotes – Gate of Warmth, Hugging, Bargains, Loyalty

40 THE GATE OF ALONENESS – DELIVERANCE

QUICK REFERENCE THEME: People who need to balance work and rest.

DESCRIPTION: One of the 3 Gates of Aloneness (40,33,12), this is the Gate of Denial.
These people are always sought after in life for the ability to work hard within a community, family or business. Traditionally, this is the hexagram of The Breadwinner. However, this gate is in the Ego Centre, of which a major theme is rest. These people therefore have to let everyone know where their boundaries lie and how much they are willing to give of themselves, as well as what they expect in return.

They can be very firm in denying other people access to their willpower. Their time alone is extremely important to them.

The 40 needs to be massaged by the understanding and loyalty of the 37 in order to get to work. If the bargain is clear, the 37 will always accommodate the 40's need for aloneness and rest whilst supporting them during the process.

ADVANCED KEYNOTES

Ego Tempering Gate – The will or lack of will to provide for the needy – the stomach
Foundation of Hexagram – 40.1 – Recuperation
Personality Sun Crosses – Planning, Denial, Migration
Genetic Codon Group – Glysine (6,47,64,40)
Awareness Stream – Stream of Sensitivity (Expression of Aloneness)
Gate of Aloneness – (40,33,12)

Gate of Love – The Love of Work
Gate of Sexuality (Emotional) – Gate of sexual denial, a design of Masturbation
Mystical Gate – The path of Denial and the pain of being alone
Nutritional – Gate of the Stomach (acid)
Other keynotes – Gate of Denial, The Weak Ego

THE MONEY LINE
A DESIGN OF A MATERIALIST

CIRCUIT: The Ego Circuit
CHANNEL TYPE: Manifested Channel

QUICK REFERENCE THEME: Yours is a life where the material plane has to be embraced fully. You are here to make money through the power of your will. It is not natural for you to work for anyone but yourself, since you are uncomfortable with others controlling you in any way.

SEXUALITY KEYNOTE: The Channel of Haves and Have-Nots.

WHOLE CHANNEL: These people are here to master the material plane. They are here to lead and be in control. The only way they can become materially successful is by doing everything themselves.

They are a one-man or one-woman show and do not work particularly well with others, as they like to do everything themselves. They are the most driven of the Manifestors if there is no sacral or solar plexus to impose a strategy of waiting. As manifestors, their natural strategy is to inform people that they need to take control before taking it.

Because this is a very powerful Ego Manifesting Channel these people can be very ego-centred. You cannot change these people! When they talk, they naturally talk about themselves. If they are not clear about their strategy, they will meet a lot of resistance, criticism and anger in others.

This channel is generally more successful as an electro-magnetic connection between two people (where the 45 is the Owner of the company and the 21 is the director who has control). However, spectacular fights can happen if the 45 tries to control the 21 or if the 21 tries to behave like the owner.

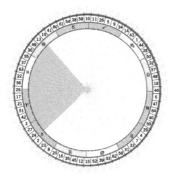

21 Quarter of Initiation
THEME: MIND

45 Quarter of Civilisation
THEME: FORM

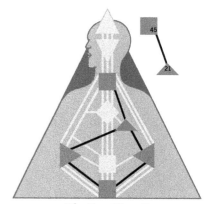

The Ego Circuit
THE MONEY LINE

THE GATE OF THE HUNTER/HUNTRESS —
BITING THROUGH

QUICK REFERENCE THEME: People who must be materially independent and who thrive when given control.

DESCRIPTION: These people have a need and a gift for being in control of the things in their life, especially money, food, territory and lifestyle.

This gate is best represented by the archetype of the managing director of a company. These are people who are at their best when they are in control of situations. They do not enjoy having anyone else tell them what to do or how to do it.

Unless they happen to be a manifestor who informs first, these are not people who can successfully assume control unless they are first offered it. More often than not, they try and take control of situations without being asked, which means that they meet fierce resistance from those they are seeking to control.

The 21 needs the patronage of the 45. The 45 represents the landowner and the 21 simply wants to be in control of the land itself without the responsibility of owning it. Without the 45, the 21 has the authority over others but lacks the overseeing presence (45) of one who is not directly involved with managing people.

ADVANCED KEYNOTES

Ego Manifesting Gate – The potential to dominate and to manage the community – "I control"
Foundation of Hexagram – 21.1 – Warning
Personality Sun Crosses – Tension, Control, Endeavour
Genetic Codon Group – Arginine (10,38,25,17,21,51)
Gate of Sexuality (Caring) – Gate of Control, a design of Care Management or not

Mystical Gate (WA) – The Hunter/Huntress
Nutritional – Diet/Thirst Command (the heart muscle)
Other keynotes – Gate of Control, The Managing Director, Shopping

THE GATE OF THE GATHERER —
GATHERING TOGETHER

QUICK REFERENCE THEME: People who are here to oversee the future and wealth of the community.

DESCRIPTION: This gate is symbolised by the archetype of the monarch. This is the autocratic tribal leader who represents the voice of the community and gives the final seal of approval to any new law.

These people are here to educate others in how to come together in more efficient ways for the benefit of the future health and wealth of the community. Their style of leadership is to govern in the traditional way simply by being at the top of the hierarchy.

The 45 always needs a prime minister (the 21) to manage their kingdom, as they don't like to get their own hands dirty! These people love to have other people working for them, running their business or helping to manage the family affairs.

ADVANCED KEYNOTES

Ego Expression Gate – Manifestation of dominance, the master or the mistress
Voice – "I/We have"
Foundation of Hexagram – 45.1 – Canvassing
Personality Sun Crosses – Rulership, Possession, Confrontation
Genetic Codon Group – Cysteine (45,16)

Gate of Sexuality (Caring) – Gate of Possession, a design of Supporting Caring or not
Mystical Gate (WA) – The Master/Mistress, The Gatherer
Nutritional – Elimination Command
Other keynotes – Gate of Education, The King/Queen, Generosity

THE CHANNEL OF MATING
DESIGN OF FOCUSED ON REPRODUCTION

CIRCUIT: The Defence Circuit (Creative Channel)
CHANNEL TYPE: Generated Channel

QUICK REFERENCE THEME: You have a very powerful auric field that penetrates people very deeply. This means that you can be intimate with almost anyone very quickly. Although this is natural for you, it is not for others, so you need to be aware of how easily you can be misunderstood.

WHOLE CHANNEL: As the Creative Channel of the Defence Circuit, this is the Gate of Pure Fertile Power. It is the demand of our genes to endlessly create more life. This is literally about making babies, but is also about birthing projects and creative processes. It is the law that life must always create life.

These people are here to penetrate others, breaking down barriers to open the way for intimacy and the birthing of new endeavours. They have very penetrating auras and can penetrate anyone's emotional defences, often without being aware that they are doing it.

The 59th gate is always available for intimacy but the 6 decides through its emotional wave patterns when and where this can happen. People who have only this channel and no other activations in the Solar Plexus have a very stable and hidden emotional wave which usually takes another person to bring it to the surface.

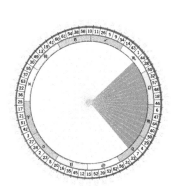

59 Quarter of Duality
THEME: RELATIONSHIPS

6 Quarter of Duality
THEME: RELATIONSHIPS

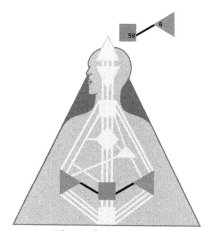

The Defence Circuit
THE CHANNEL OF MATING

THE GATE OF SEXUALITY — DISPERSION

QUICK REFERENCE THEME: People who are driven by their genes to reproduce, whether that be children or creative endeavours.

DESCRIPTION: Manifesting as the desire to be sexually intimate, this gate determines our individual sexual strategy for attracting the best mate (look at the six lines of the 59 to see the six different strategies: 1 – The Preemptive Strike, 2 – Shyness, 3 – Openness, 4 – Brotherhood/Sisterhood, 5 – The Femme Fatale/Casanova, 6 – The one night stand).

These people must wait to respond rather than jumping into bonds prematurely, otherwise they simply stay on the surface of intimacy rather than penetrating to the core of another being. This is a Gate of Fertility that when connected to the 6, strongly increases the likelihood of conception. This archetype is about sex and intimacy rather than marriage.

The 59 needs the boundaries of the 6 in order to decide when and with whom intimacy can take place.

ADVANCED KEYNOTES

Sexual Role Gate – Sexual power, fertility, reproductive strategies
Foundation of Hexagram – 59.1 – The Preemptive strike
Personality Sun Crosses – Sleeping Phoenix, Strategy, Spirit
Genetic Codon Group – Valine (59,29,4,7)

Gate of Sexuality (Emotional) – Gate of Genetic Imperative, a design of the Role in Sexual Bonding
Mystical Gate (WA) – The Binder – Power of Fertility
Other keynotes – Gate of the Aura Breaker, Penetration, Intimacy

THE GATE OF FRICTION — CONFLICT

QUICK REFERENCE THEME: People who are designed to be discriminating emotionally and sexually.

DESCRIPTION: These people are here to learn to control the flood of emotions through the Solar Plexus. This gate is like a border guard that governs when we are open or closed to intimacy. It also compresses all the potential streams of awareness and emotional waves from the Solar Plexus Centre (look at the six lines of the 6 to see the six different themes of intimacy: 1 – Retreat, 2 – The Guerilla, 3 – Allegiance, 4 – Triumph, 5 – Arbitration, 6 – The Peacemaker).

The 6 needs the 59 to provide the energy to break down barriers to intimacy, excitement and reproduction.

ADVANCED KEYNOTES

Awareness Compression Gate – Awareness of whether to bond or not
Foundation of Hexagram – 6.1 – Retreat
Personality Sun Crosses – Eden, Conflict, Plane
Genetic Codon Group – Glysine (6,47,64,40)
Gate of Sexuality (Caring) – Gate of The Builder, a design of being Intimate or not

Gate of Fear – The Fear of Intimacy
Gate of Nervousness – Nervousness over being open to others
Mystical Gate (WA) – The Regulator – Builder
Nutritional – PH Balance
Other keynotes – Gate of the Skin

27/50 THE CHANNEL OF PRESERVATION
A DESIGN OF CUSTODIANSHIP
CIRCUIT: The Defence Circuit
CHANNEL TYPE: Generated Channel

QUICK REFERENCE THEME: You are someone who is here to either maintain or change the values of the people in the community around you. Added to this, you have an aura that generates automatic trust from others, which means that people look to you naturally for support. The only lesson you have to learn is not to take on so much responsibility that you lose sight of yourself.

WHOLE CHANNEL: As part of the Defence Circuit, this channel is about nurturing our offspring and guiding them through correct values in order to maintain a high standard of living within the community. Ultimately, this is about the preservation of our genetic lineage.

These people are natural nurturers, providers and leaders. Their sacral responses will always lead them to feel certain responsibilities for others, or not. Because of the power of the Defence Circuit, these people naturally pull others into their aura in order to establish or undermine certain values, and because of their aura, others naturally trust in them. They always have the power to bring attention to the values or lack of values around them. They can even catch the attention and conscience of the most selfish individuals and outsiders, bringing them into the 'community'.

These are people who preserve the infrastructure of our communities – e.g: police, lawyers, therapists – anything from cooks to crooks!

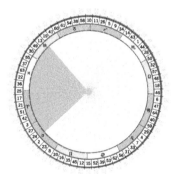

27 Quarter of Initiation
THEME: MIND

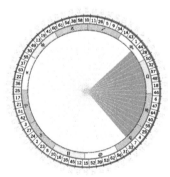

50 Quarter of Duality
THEME: RELATIONSHIPS

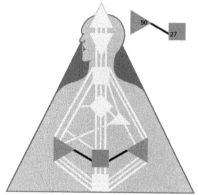

The Defence Circuit
THE CHANNEL OF PRESERVATION

THE GATE OF CARING – NOURISHMENT

QUICK REFFRENCE THEME: People who are here to preserve and protect themselves and/or others.

DESCRIPTION: People with this gate defined are here to learn about how to take care of themselves and/or others. At its most exalted, this is the Gate of Compassion. However, these people can very easily end up sacrificing themselves and their own wellbeing for the sake of others.

The first line of this gate is actually called 'Selfishness', which is the foundation of all caring – to take care of yourself first, otherwise you can be of no use to others (look at the six lines of the 27 to see the six archetypal caring roles: 1 – Selfishness, 2 – Self-sufficiency, 3 – Greed, 4 – Generosity, 5 – The Executor, 6 – Wariness).

Because this is a Sacral Gate, these people don't know who or what it is they care for unless they wait to respond, rather than rush into taking care of everything and anyone, or indeed, no one.

Without the 50, these people have an impulse to care for others, but lack the instinct to set healthy boundaries around their impulse.

ADVANCED KEYNOTES

Caring Role Gate – Nourishment, the power to care, the potential for compassion
Foundation of Hexagram – 27.1 – Selfishness
Personality Sun Crosses – Unexpected, Caring, Alignment
Genetic Codon Group – Leucine (42,3,27,24,20,23)
Gate of Sexuality (Caring) – Gate of Genetic Imperative, a design of the Role of Caring

Mystical Gate (WA) – The Mother/Father
Dreamrave Key – Yearning (Earth Plane)
Design of Forms – Sexuality – Communal Altruism (Mammals)
Other keynotes – Gate of Compassion/Selfishness

THE GATE OF VALUES – THE CAULDRON

QUICK REFERENCE THEME: People who are here to establish or challenge values or responsibilities within the community.

DESCRIPTION: These people have an inbuilt responsibility to the community and people around them. They are here to uphold or challenge the laws that govern the preservation and well-being of the community. Since this gate represents the potential fear of responsibility, these people can also be law breakers or challengers of the established law.

Like the 6th gate, this is a complex gate. It compresses all the streams of awareness that run through the Spleen Centre. In the ancient chinese I Ching, this hexagram was represented by a cauldron, where all the values of society are synthesised. Anyone who has this gate is a potential guardian or stirrer of the values within their community.

Without the 27, these people are here to take responsibility for people without necessarily having to look after them. The 50 needs the balance of the 27 and its gift of caring.

ADVANCED KEYNOTES

Awareness Compression Gate – Awareness to be responsible or not
Foundation of Hexagram – 50.1 – The Immigrant
Personality Sun Crosses – Laws, Values, Wishes
Genetic Codon Group – Glutamic Acid (44,50)
Gate of Sexuality (Caring) – Gate of The Guardian, a design of Caring or not

Gate of Fear – The Fear of Responsibility
Mystical Gate (WA) – The Enforcer/Guardian
Dreamrave Key – Sex (Earth Plane)
Design of Forms – The Herd Instinct/The Guardian (mammals)
Other keynotes – Gate of Trustworthiness, Cooking

other books by Richard Rudd

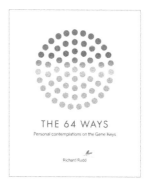

Living Your Design
(coming soon)

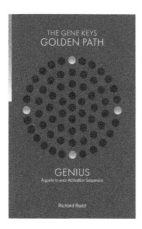

CPSIA information can be obtained
at www.ICGtesting.com
Printed in the USA
LVHW070830210722
723938LV00010B/36

9 781999 671051